Therapeutic Exercises for Children: Guided Self-Discovery Using Cognitive-Behavioral Techniques

Robert D. Friedberg
Barbara A. Friedberg
Rebecca J. Friedberg

Professional Resource Press
Sarasota, Florida

D1511818

Published by Professional Resource Press
(An imprint of Professional Resource Exchange, Inc.)
Post Office Box 3197
Sarasota, FL 34230-3197

The copy editor was Brian Fogarty, the managing editor was Debbie Fink, the production coordinator was Laurie Girsch, the graphics designer was Bob Lefebvre, and Carol Tornatore created the cover.

Library of Congress Catloging-in-Publication Data

Friedberg, Robert D., date.
     Therapeutic exercises for children : guided self-discovery using cognitive-behavioral
techniques / Robert D. Friedberg, Barbara A. Friedberg, Rebecca J. Friedberg
       p. cm.
     Includes bibliographical references.
     ISBN-13: 978-1-56887-065-6
     ISBN-10: 1-56887-065-5
     1. Anxiety in children--Treatment--Problems, exercises, etc. 2. Cognitive therapy for
children--Problems, exercises, etc. 3. Children--Mental health services--Problems,
exercises, etc. 4. Self-perception--Problems, exercises, etc. I. Friedberg, Barbara A., date.
II. Friedberg, Rebecca J. III. Title.

RJ506.A58 F753 2001
618.92'89142--dc21

                                  00-045674

Dedications

This workbook is dedicated to my parents, Morton and Rachelle, who encouraged my creativity.

RDF

I dedicate this book to my parents, Helen and Harry, who taught me that with hard work and determination anything is possible.

BAF

I dedicate this book to my parents who helped me when I was feeling blue and always turned a bad day into a good one just by smiling.

RJF

Acknowledgments

My co-authors deserve much credit for tolerating my editorial style. I wish to acknowledge the faculty and students at Wright State University, School of Professional Psychology and especially the many doctoral-trainees who participated in the PANDY Program. Further, I want to thank the faculty and administrations of Five Points, Moraine Meadows, and Loos Elementary Schools. Finally, I want to thank the parents and children who were served in the PANDY Program.

RDF

I acknowledge my husband, Robert Friedberg, whose generosity and encouragement has provided me with momentous opportunity. Rebecca, my most precious daughter, has deepened my understanding of the child's world. Finally, I thank Dr. Larry Ritt, Ms. Debra Fink, and Ms. Laurie Girsch for their support and precise communication throughout this project.

BAF

Thanks to my 5th grade teachers, Mrs. Bridget Fiore, Mr. Chris Fisher, and Mr. Eric Snead, who without their endless dedication, I wouldn't have persevered through my writing.

RJF

Table of Contents

PRIMING EXERCISES

SELF-INSTRUCTIONAL METHODS

TECHNIQUES REQUIRING MORE IN-DEPTH RATIONAL ANALYSIS

Therapeutic Exercises for Children: Guided Self-Discovery Using Cognitive-Behavioral Techniques

Introduction

DESCRIPTION OF THE WORKBOOK

Therapeutic Exercises for Children: Guided Self-Discovery Using Cognitive-Behavioral Techniques is a set of well-constructed cognitive-behavioral coping skills for children ages 8 to 11 years old who are experiencing depressed and anxious mood states. The material is based on cognitive-behavioral theory and therapy. Moreover, many of the exercises were initially developed at the Preventing Anxiety and Depression in Youth (PANDY) Program at the Wright State University School of Professional Psychology in Dayton, Ohio. A mouse cartoon is a central figure in the exercises. The mouse is called PANDY and each exercise includes PANDY's "Tips for Children." Each skill set includes a section providing "Guidelines for Therapists," "Tips for Children," and the exercise itself. The workbook contains many exercises and it is not expected that every child will complete every worksheet. The therapist will need to tailor the treatment to particular children. The *Therapeutic Exercises for Children: Professional Guide* will be especially helpful in helping therapists flexibly apply the workbook exercises to different children's treatment needs. In this introduction to the workbook, we will briefly describe the theoretical foundation of the workbook, explain its contents and layout, and explicate its usefulness.

THEORETICAL MODEL

Therapeutic Exercises for Children is based on cognitive theory and psychotherapy as espoused by Aaron T. Beck, MD (A. T. Beck, 1976, 1985; A. T. Beck et al., 1979). Moreover, the workbook is also based on the seminal work done in applying cognitive-behavioral therapy to children completed by Kendall and his colleagues (Kendall et al., 1992), Seligman and his colleagues (Seligman et al., 1995), as well as Silverman and Kurtines (1996). Basically, a cognitive-behavioral model posits that four symptom clusters emerge in psychologically meaningful environments. These four symptom clusters include physiological changes, behavioral changes, emotional changes, and cognitive changes. The four symptom clusters are causally interrelated such that by making a change in one symptom cluster, change in the remaining three is realized (A. T. Beck, 1985). Typically, a distressing event in a child's context triggers these symptoms (e.g., divorce, going to school, peer rejection, etc.).

Cognitive-behavioral therapy identifies behavioral and cognitive symptoms as initial treatment targets. Accordingly, cognitive therapy aims interventions directly toward cognitive-behavioral symptoms as a way to change physiological and affective distress. Not surprisingly then, the workbook exercises emphasize action and thinking patterns. The focus is on guiding children to identify their stressors and experiment with new ways of thinking and doing. Cognitive therapy helps youngsters acquire and apply coping skills. The coping skills are presented in a lively, experiential, and here-and-now manner. In this way, the skills become more real for the youngsters. The *Therapeutic Exercises for Children: Professional Guide* offers numerous recommendations for augmenting the experiential nature of the cognitive skills. Finally, homework is an essential component of a cognitive-behavioral approach to treatment. It is expected that therapists will collaboratively assign portions of the workbook exercises to children for homework. The **Memory Jogger** exercise provides a chart to keep track of the child's homework (or mousework) assignments.

Purchasers of this book may photocopy and/or adapt these exercises solely for use with their clients in therapeutic settings. Further information about copyright exceptions may be found on page ii of this workbook. Although page numbers are printed on the bottom of each page to simplify searches for particular exercises, some purchasers may wish to delete these numbers on copies of exercises reproduced for use with their clients.

Therapeutic Exercises for Children is divided into four sections: self-monitoring exercises, priming exercises, self-instructional/self-control exercises, and rational analysis exercises. Generally, therapists will begin with a self-monitoring task, proceed to priming exercises, and then progress to self-instructional and rational analysis techniques. The "Guidelines for Therapists" section, which precedes each exercise, is designed to guide the therapist's decision-making. Additionally, the *Therapeutic Exercises for Children: Professional Guide* will promote therapists' mindful selection of appropriate techniques.

The self-monitoring section includes **Diamond Connections**, **PANDY Coloring Sheet**, **PANDY Fun Diary**, **Memory Jogger**, **My Mouse Traps and PANDY Fix-It**, **Bubble Up Your Fear**, and **Catching Feelings and Thoughts**. All of these exercises teach children ways to identify their distressing thoughts, feelings, bodily reactions, behavioral patterns, and situational circumstances. **My Mouse Traps and PANDY Fix-It** includes a problem-solving component and the **PANDY Fun Diary** offers a way to increase their daily pleasant events. All the activities refer to the PANDY mouse cartoon and include "Tips for Children" which explain the various tasks to youngsters.

Once children apply their self-monitoring skills to their problems, they are ready for priming tasks. Priming tasks are designed to prepare the children for the self-instructional and rational analysis techniques. The theoretical and clinical background of priming procedures is briefly discussed in the "Guidelines for Therapists" sections and further explicated in the *Therapeutic Exercises for Children: Professional Guide*. The workbook includes three priming tasks: **Permanent or Temporary**, **Sticks and Stones**, and **Many Meanings**. **Permanent or Temporary** works to shift children's viewpoint from believing most events are unchangeable to the perspective that most circumstances are temporary. **Sticks and Stones** is designed for attenuating the effects of pernicious self-criticisms. **Many Meanings** primes children to think from alternative perspectives.

The self-instructional skills follow the priming techniques. There are four self-instructional tools: **Me/Not Me**, **Changing Your Tune**, **Tease Whiz**, and **Surf the Angry Sea**. **Changing Your Tune** is the most general technique and can be applied to a variety of situations. **Changing Your Tune** is a modification of a classic self-instructional tool (Meichenbaum, 1985). **Me/Not Me** is a self-instructional drill which should be used with children who assume excessive responsibility for circumstances which are beyond their control. **Tease Whiz** offers several skills to youngsters who are the objects of teasing. Finally, **Surf the Angry Sea** coaches children to apply self-instructional tools to angry feelings.

The final section of the workbook includes techniques emphasizing rational analysis. There are four rational analysis exercises including **Clue Snooping**, **Real or False Alarms**, **Breaking the Crystal Ball**, and **Thought Digger**. The rational analysis techniques require more depthful processing and more sophisticated reasoning abilities. **Real or False Alarms** is the most specific exercise and is designed to help children discern which of their worries are realistic and which worries are merely inaccurate catastrophic predictions. **Breaking the Crystal Ball** is also a technique designed to attenuate children's inaccurate predictions. **Clue Snooping** and **Thought Digger** are more general cognitive therapy exercises which are applicable to a wide range of emotional distress. **Clue Snooping** is a modification of a traditional test of evidence and **Thought Digger** teaches children questions to ask themselves to evaluate the accuracy of their thinking.

HOW THIS WORKBOOK CAN BE USEFUL

Therapeutic Exercises for Children is a handy aid for mental health professionals entrusted with the care of children ages 8 to 11 years old who are experiencing depressed and anxious mood states. The workbook consists of well-crafted exercises that guide therapists' work with children. The exercises focus on skill development. The activities readily fit into experienced cognitive-behavioral therapists' repertoires. Additionally, the workbook helps the novice cognitive therapist scaffold Socratic dialogues and behavioral experiments, which propel guided discovery. Finally, the *Therapeutic Exercises for Children: Professional Guide* provides further clinical direction, and promotes depthful management of various clinical vicissitudes associated with childhood depression and anxiety.

Self-Monitoring Exercises

Diamond Connections

GUIDELINES FOR THERAPISTS

A critical first step in cognitive-behavioral therapy is educating clients about the treatment model (A. T. Beck et al., 1979; Padesky & Greenberger, 1995). Socialization to the treatment model demystifies therapy and gives children a map for understanding treatment. Many explanations of therapy for youngsters are dull, boring, and frequently go over children's heads.

Diamond Connections is a simple and entertaining tool used for socializing children to the cognitive model. A baseball diamond is offered as a metaphor and includes the central parts of the cognitive model as bases. Feelings, actions, bodily reactions, and thoughts are represented on the diamond. Their connections are self-evident because all four bases are necessary parts of a baseball diamond.

Reviewing the "Tips for Children" is a good first step. The programmed steps in the "Tips" text facilitates interactive teaching. Therapists and children should read the passages aloud, pausing to process salient points. The "Tips" provide a conceptual template for categorizing and distinguishing between thoughts, feelings, bodily reactions, and behavioral actions. When coupled with the sample worksheet, which is completed in a child's handwriting, the child should gain a robust introduction to therapy.

The worksheet begins at first base (feelings). The child is invited to share all the different words she/he uses to express scared or sad feelings. Certainly, children are allowed to use the sample words supplied by the examples on the worksheet and sample worksheet. However, a better option is including more words that the children personally use to tell others they are sad or scared. In this way, the feeling words become more contextually valid.

The worksheet continues around the bases (actions, thoughts, and bodily reactions). At each base, children are asked to supply personal examples. When children have worked their way around the diamond, the therapists can explain the **Diamond Connections.**

Therapists can enliven this exercise in several ways. For instance, children could stand on bases while they express their feelings, thoughts, actions, and behaviors. In our school-based group work, the children were invited to pass bases among each other and tell their particular symptoms to each other. The group leaders can pretend to be a public address announcer exclaiming, "On second base is Tommy, and Tommy is going to tell us what things he does when he is sad."

Diamond Connections ties together the basic tenets of cognitive-behavioral therapy into a playful metaphor familiar to children. The baseball diamond illustrates the interrelationship between thoughts, feelings, actions, and bodily sensations. Further, just like in a baseball diamond, **Diamond Connections** shows that one base of the tenets cannot exist without the others. Finally, this basic exercise teaches the children the beginning steps in identifying thoughts, feelings, actions, and bodily sensations.

Diamond Connections

Tips for Children

Hi, boys and girls. I am going to show you how your thoughts, actions, feelings, and bodily changes are connected. I was in a maze looking for some cheese. I was kind of <u>excited</u> and <u>my body felt tingly</u> and <u>on edge</u>. I said to myself, "I really want some cheese. I hope I can find it quickly." Take a look at where I am on my diamond.

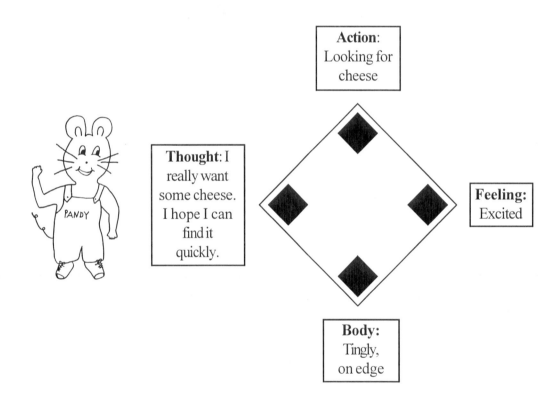

I started into the maze and turned corner upon corner. After a few twists and turns, I was lost. I began to feel worried and started to sweat. My mouth felt dry and my throat felt like there was a lump in it. My stomach started to hurt. The following thoughts went through my mind: "Oh no, I've made a terrible, stupid mistake. I'm lost and I'll never find my way to the cheese. Every step I take is a mistake. I'm trapped." I could not think straight and make choices. I was stuck and I stopped trying to find my way.

See if you can figure out what goes on at each base now.

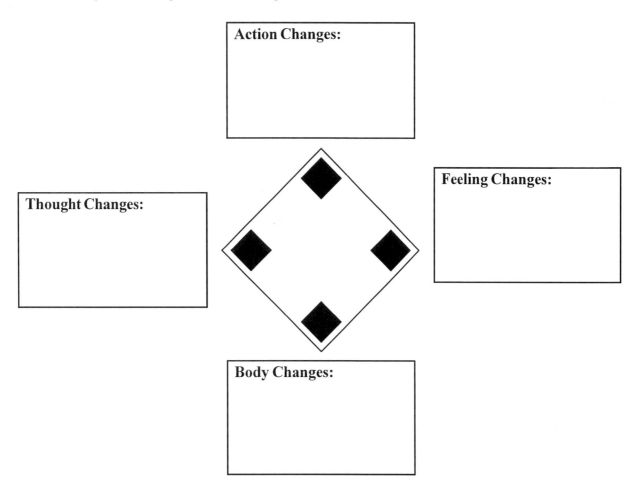

So, there I was, stuck in a corner of the maze trying to find some cheese. My stomach started to turn over and around and over again. My head started to pound "Thump, thump," and hurt.

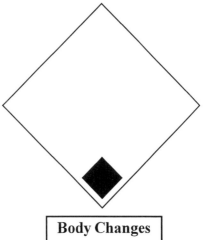

I began to feel sad and worried.

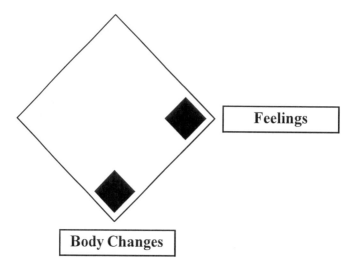

I didn't know what to do. I gave up trying to find a way out of the maze. I sat down in the corner and started to cry.

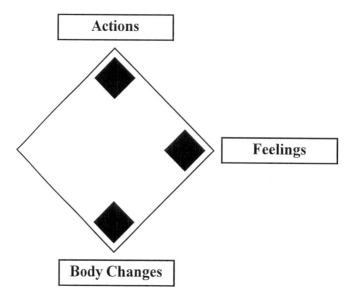

I thought, "What's the use. I'm stupid. I'll never figure things out. The cheese is not really important to me anyway. People will be very disappointed in me."

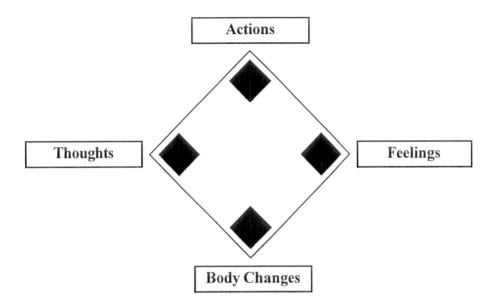

My body, thoughts, actions, and feelings were all connected. They were all tied together. One part could not move without the other one.

Then, I stopped crying and looked around. I began exploring some of the paths in the maze. Sure, some were blocked, but others led to more paths. What part of my **Diamond Connections** changed (circle one)?

Action   Thinking   Feeling   Body

As I started exploring and trying out new paths, I started to feel differently. My sad and worried feelings started to change. My stomach was not as "jumpy" as before and my head didn't hurt as much. And you know what? Thoughts like, "I'm stupid and nothing will work out for me," stopped going through my mind. As I walked and explored more, I found my way out of the maze and reached the cheese. And you know what? The cheese sure was tasty!

I hope my example gave you some ideas about using my **Diamond Connections Worksheet**. Take a look at my sample worksheet.

Diamond Connections Worksheet

(Sample)

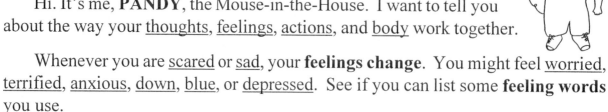

Hi. It's me, **PANDY**, the Mouse-in-the-House. I want to tell you about the way your <u>thoughts</u>, <u>feelings</u>, <u>actions</u>, and <u>body</u> work together.

Whenever you are <u>scared</u> or <u>sad</u>, your **feelings change**. You might feel <u>worried</u>, <u>terrified</u>, <u>anxious</u>, <u>down</u>, <u>blue</u>, or <u>depressed</u>. See if you can list some **feeling words** you use.

Scared Words	Sad Words
Scared	down
Worried	sad
frightened	blue
Jittery	gloomy

You may have some changes in your **body** when you are scared and sad. Your <u>stomach might get upset</u>, you have <u>headaches</u>, you <u>sweat</u> a lot even when it is not hot, you get <u>dizzy</u>, or you have <u>trouble sleeping</u>. List some changes you notice in your **body**.

How my body is when I am scared	How my body is when I am sad
My body feels tight.	I feel tired.
My throat is dry.	I get a headache.
My hands sweat.	I get a stomachache.

There are things you do when you are scared and sad. Sometimes <u>when you are sad</u>, you don't have as much fun doing the things you used to like, you give up on things faster, or you get into more fights with family and friends. When you are scared, you might have more nightmares or bad dreams, you may become more shy around other people, or you stay away from things that scare you like school or dogs or elevators. See if you can list some of the things you do when you are **scared** and **sad**.

12

Things I do when I am scared	Things I do when I am sad
I let other kids tell me what to do.	I cry.
I get very quiet.	I stay by myself.
I have trouble falling asleep.	I give up on things.
I have trouble getting ready for school.	I act grumpy.

There are things <u>you say to yourself</u> when you are scared or sad. These things are called your **thoughts**. Your **thoughts** might be things like, "I'm ugly. I'm no good. I'll never feel like I fit in. All the kids will think I'm weird. Being in school is scary. I'm going to embarrass myself." List some **thoughts** you have.

Thoughts I have when I am scared	Thoughts I have when I am sad
Something bad is going to happen.	I'm stupid.
I can't handle this.	I'm ugly.
Being scared + nervous is awful.	Nobody likes me.
Other kids will think I'm weird.	I will never fit in.

These **thoughts**, **feelings**, **actions**, and **body** changes all happen together. They are connected in kind of a diamond shape. Here's how it looks.

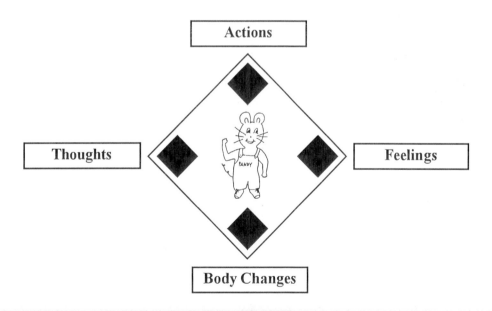

We are going to work on all the diamonds to help you feel better.

Diamond Connections Worksheet

Hi. It's me, **PANDY**, the Mouse-in-the-House. I want to tell you about the way your <u>thoughts</u>, <u>feelings</u>, <u>actions</u>, and <u>body</u> work together.

Whenever you are <u>scared</u> or <u>sad</u>, your **feelings change**. You might feel <u>worried</u>, <u>terrified</u>, <u>anxious</u>, <u>down</u>, <u>blue</u>, or <u>depressed</u>. See if you can list some **feeling words** you use.

Scared Words	Sad Words

You may have some changes in your **body** when you are scared and sad. Your <u>stomach might get upset</u>, you have <u>headaches</u>, you <u>sweat</u> a lot even when it is not hot, you get <u>dizzy</u>, or you have <u>trouble sleeping</u>. List some changes you notice in your **body**.

How my body is when I am scared	How my body is when I am sad

There are things you do when you are scared and sad. Sometimes <u>when you are sad</u>, you don't have as much fun doing the things you used to like, you give up on things faster, or you get into more fights with family and friends. When you are scared, you might have more nightmares or bad dreams, you may become more shy around other people, or you stay away from things that scare you like school or dogs or elevators. See if you can list some of the things you do when you are **scared** and **sad**.

Things I do when I am scared	Things I do when I am sad

There are things <u>you say to yourself</u> when you are scared or sad. These things are called your **thoughts**. Your **thoughts** might be things like, "I'm ugly. I'm no good. I'll never feel like I fit in. All the kids will think I'm weird. Being in school is scary. I'm going to embarrass myself." List some **thoughts** you have.

Thoughts I have when I am scared	Thoughts I have when I am sad

These **thoughts**, **feelings**, **actions**, and **body** changes all happen together. They are connected in kind of a diamond shape. Here's how it looks.

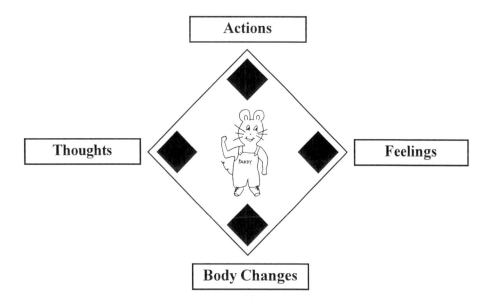

We are going to work on all the diamonds to help you feel better.

PANDY
Coloring Sheet

GUIDELINES FOR THERAPISTS

The **PANDY Coloring Sheet** is a simple and fun way to introduce therapy in general and the cognitive-behavioral model in particular to children. The coloring sheet has a large PANDY picture waving to the child. PANDY is missing a feeling face in the picture and children are invited to color in PANDY's outline. When they have different feelings over the week, they are asked to draw the type of face that goes along with the feeling. For example, if they feel sad, they might draw a face on PANDY that reflects a sad feeling. Finally, they are asked to write the name of the feeling they draw on PANDY and the date in the space below the picture. The counselors and therapists can ask the children to fill out a **PANDY Coloring Sheet** each time they have a strong feeling. You are welcome to reproduce the **PANDY Coloring Sheet** for the children.

The **PANDY Coloring Sheet** is a basic self-monitoring task. When the children complete the skills over the week, therapists may gain a glimpse into the frequency and variety of the types of feelings the child experiences over the week. For instance, if the child has predominantly happy faces with only one sad face and one worried face the first week, the therapist has a baseline from which to work. If the child presents the next week with one sad face, one worried face, and one happy face, the therapist has a prior baseline from which to compare. The change in the child's pattern of feelings can be a useful starting point for therapeutic exploration.

The **PANDY Coloring Sheet** is a *simple* and *nonthreatening introduction to therapy*. The task allows the child to identify and share the feelings in a familiar manner. Most children have plenty of experience coloring pictures and drawing faces on characters. The **PANDY Coloring Sheet** also provides *socialization* to the treatment model and the PANDY icon. By coloring the mouse character, they become familiar with the PANDY character. The identification process begins as the children put their feeling faces on PANDY. Further, *the objectification process is promoted*. When the children draw the faces that represent their feelings, they begin to externalize their internal subjective experiences. As the children transform their subjective internal experiences into outward objective expressions, they distance themselves from the inner experiences. This distancing process allows the child to explore their feelings from another more objective perspective.

Occasionally, children may complete the PANDY assignment by drawing all positive, happy faces. If a child draws all one type of face each time the task is assigned, further investigation is warranted. Children may be reluctant to report negative feelings for a variety of reasons. Accordingly, therapists need to develop and check out numerous hypotheses (e.g., "Is the child worried about disclosing the feelings due to fears of loss of control? Does the child possess personal prohibitions regarding talking about negative feelings? Does the child's home environment support emotional expression?").

Therapists can use the **PANDY Coloring Sheet** as a stimulus for checking out these hypotheses. For instance, therapists might draw a sad face on PANDY and ask questions such as:

- "Does your face ever look like this?"
- "Can you make your face look like this?"
- "What type of feeling face is this?"
- "What is it like to share _____ feelings with me?"
- "Who else do you tell your _____ feelings to?"

In this way, the therapist begins to normalize emotional expression.

The **PANDY Coloring Sheet** can also be used to make paper sandwich-bag puppets. For example, the **PANDY Coloring Sheet** could be cut out and pasted on a paper sandwich bag. The children and therapist could then enjoy puppet play with the PANDY sandwich-bag puppets. The sandwich-bag puppets can be integrated with many of the skills in the *Therapeutic Exercises for Children Workbook.*

The **PANDY Coloring Sheet** can serve as a baseline and simple monitoring tool of children's feelings. It is a fun, convenient, and educational tool which introduces the *Therapeutic Exercises for Children Workbook.* The drawing and coloring task is a familiar one to children. The **PANDY Coloring Sheet** "sets the table" for many of the more advanced skills which follow in the *Therapeutic Exercises for Children Workbook.*

PANDY
Coloring Sheet

Tips for Children

PANDY SAYS

Hello, boys and girls. I'm **PANDY**, the Mouse-in-the-House. You will see me on the worksheets I wrote for this workbook. What do you think of the picture of me? I would like you to color me in. Use any colors you want.

Do you notice that there is a part of my face missing on the **PANDY Coloring Sheet**? What part is it? That's right, my mouth is missing. I want you to draw my mouth. Here's what you do.

Whenever you have a feeling this week, I want you to draw your feeling face on my picture. If you were feeling happy, what feeling face would you draw? Go ahead and draw it on my face. If you were sad, what feeling face would you draw? Go ahead and draw that face on another **PANDY Coloring Sheet**. Write down the name of the feeling above it. Write the date below the picture. Look at my drawing if you get stuck. You have got the idea!

Talk to your counselor and decide how many **PANDY Coloring Sheets** to complete.

PANDY Coloring Sheet

(Sample)

Write down the feeling you are feeling right now: <u>Sad</u>.

Draw **PANDY'S** mouth and color **PANDY** in to show how you are feeling.

Date:
Nov. 15

PANDY Coloring Sheet

Write down the feeling you are feeling right now: _____.

Draw **PANDY'S** mouth and color **PANDY** in to show how you are feeling.

Date:

21

PANDY Fun Diary

GUIDELINES FOR THERAPISTS

PANDY Fun Diary is the worksheet designed for pleasant activity scheduling. Pleasant activity scheduling is a core cognitive-behavioral treatment technique designed to increase the frequency of pleasant events (A. T. Beck et al., 1979). In pleasant activity scheduling, children list the activities they enjoy doing and then plan to do them. The **PANDY Fun Diary** simplifies pleasant event scheduling for youngsters. The **PANDY Fun Diary** is a useful strategy early in treatment and can precede the cognitive skills training. Moreover, the **PANDY Fun Diary** can be used to activate inert youngsters and the increased level of positive reinforcement may more fully engage them in treatment.

Adult pleasant activity schedules tend to be more complex and detailed (A. T. Beck et al., 1979; Greenberger & Padesky, 1995). For instance, most of the hours in the day are listed on an adult worksheet. The **PANDY Fun Diary** simplifies the task by asking the child to note only whether they accomplished the activity in the morning, afternoon, or night, whereas adults are typically asked to write down the activity (e.g., going to a movie). Writing down the activity is a relatively complex task demand. Accordingly, in the **PANDY Fun Diary**, children are asked only to place a sticker in the box that corresponds to the time of day they attempted the fun activity. Colorful dot stickers are very handy for this technique. The adhesive dots come in different colors and different sizes and children can easily stick them in the appropriate spot. Additionally, the dots could be color coded by the child to represent various activities (e.g., red = watching TV, blue = bike riding, etc.). For children who have trouble remembering the code, the therapist and child could "preprint" each label by briefly marking a notation on several labels. For example, they could write "b-ball" on several red stickers to represent playing basketball.

The "Tips for Children" text is a useful way to introduce the task and explain the rationale to children. Therapists should read over the text with the child and make sure the youngsters understand the task. Explaining the connection between increased pleasant activity and increased mood is a good idea. Therapists might ask the children if they notice that they are less interested in things they used to enjoy and have less fun when doing these activities when they feel depressed.

Distressed youngsters may have difficulty coming up with pleasant activities. In this case, therapists have several options. The literature includes several pleasant events surveys which list typical enjoyable activities for children (Daley, 1969; Phillips, Fischer, & Singh, 1977). The child simply reads the list and checks whether they have enjoyed these activities. The marked activities represent the children's choice of pleasant events. Stark (1990) includes several such surveys for each grade level.

An alternative to "canned" events is directly asking the child and parent about pleasant events. For children who are having difficulty coming up with items, therapists might ask, "What did you do for fun before you felt sad?" Another strategy is simply to ask parents to record and count the frequency of the child's activities. This baseline information will give therapists information on the things that the child does frequently. Many of these most frequent activities might be considered pleasant and reinforcing. Finally, therapists may invite the child and parents to review a local newspaper and then select activities that seem fun, accessible, cost efficient, and doable. For example, there might be a festival in the park, a free nature walk, or a museum activity for children listed in the local newspaper. Once they have made these selections, they can cut the activities out of the newspaper and place them in a box or jar. Then, the family makes a commitment to select activities from the cookie jar several times a week. Both children and parents may enjoy scheduling these fun activities and following through with them.

There are several other more advanced uses for the **PANDY Fun Diary**. Therapists might add before and after mood ratings to the activities. For instance, the child could experiment with inviting a friend over to her house. The child might rate how she feels before the invitation, and then rate how she feels after they play together.

The **PANDY Fun Diary** can also be used to record children's exposure trials or challenging and fearful activities. The child could place a sticker in the spot representing a time when they challenged themselves with an exposure trial. For instance, if they asked a friend to play at recess on a Tuesday afternoon, they could put a sticker dot in the space for the Tuesday afternoon. Therapists, parents, and children could "pre-print" the dots noting the tasks on the label (e.g., talking to a friend at recess, say hello to a friend, asking someone their name). Different color sticker dots could represent different activities.

Pleasant activity scheduling is an important component in treating depression. By regularly incorporating fun activities into a child's routine, there is less opportunity to experience depressive feelings. Frequently, the family also benefits from incorporating more fun into their schedule. Finally, the therapist can tailor the use of the **PANDY Fun Diary** according to the needs of the child and family.

PANDY Fun Diary

Tips for Children

PANDY SAYS

Do you like to have fun? I do. I bet that when you are sad or worried, you are not having fun. One thing I want to do is to boost your fun.

I made up this **Fun Diary**. It is a way for you to find time to do more fun things that may make you feel better about yourself. How does that sound?

Here's what you do. Think up as many things that are fun for you as you can. Talk to your parents and counselors to come up with more ideas. Write down all the fun things you came up with on a separate piece of paper or in the "Notes" part. Next, make a plan to do at least one or two fun things each day. When you do them, write them down on my **PANDY Fun Diary** to keep track.

The "Notes" part at the bottom of the diary can be used in any way you want. You might write down which activities you liked the best. You could also note how you felt after doing a fun activity.

PANDY Fun Diary

(Sample)

PANDY SAYS

Do two fun things a day.

Put a sticker in the box when you do it.

PANDY

	MONDAY	TUESDAY	WEDNESDAY	THURSDAY	FRIDAY	SATURDAY	SUNDAY
MORNING						bike	read
AFTERNOON	TV	play toys		TV / friend		soccer	play with dog
NIGHT	bike	ball	play toys / play cards		movie / ice cream		

Notes:

Pandy Fun Diary

PANDY SAYS

Do two fun things a day.

Put a sticker in the box when you do it.

	MONDAY	TUESDAY	WEDNESDAY	THURSDAY	FRIDAY	SATURDAY	SUNDAY
MORNING							
AFTERNOON							
NIGHT							

Notes:

Memory Jogger

GUIDELINES FOR THERAPISTS

Homework is a central part of cognitive-behavioral therapy. Clinical experience suggests that many children do not remember their homework tasks. Accordingly, they need a handy memory aid that jogs their recall. **Memory Jogger** is a form for the youngsters to record their mousework (homework). The form has a place for the date and lines where children can write out their assignment. Whenever a mousework task is assigned, the children record it on the **Memory Jogger**.

It is recommended that therapists introduce the **Memory Jogger** in a lively and fun manner. Therapists may introduce the sheet through the jogger image. The therapist might say,

- "Do you know what a jogger is?"
- "What do they look like when they jog?"
- "Now I want you to try to think about what your jogger looks like. How does your jogger run?"

At this point, therapists may want to have the child pretend to jog in place. Tying the concept to a physical action may increase retention.

After the child has demonstrated the jogger, the therapist can playfully refer to the image whenever mousework is assigned. Additionally, therapists could place a sticker alongside the mousework assignment completed for each session. Parents could be taught to check mousework and initial the completion of the work or put a sticker alongside the assignment.

The **Memory Jogger** is a light-hearted way to record mousework assignments. The **Memory Jogger** reminds children to keep track of their assignments. Additionally, **Memory Jogger** serves as a place where therapists and parents can reinforce children's coping efforts. Finally, completing the **Memory Jogger** emphasizes the notion that the skills require practice.

Memory Jogger

Tips for Children

PANDY SAYS

I sometimes forget to use my **PANDY** tools. I wanted a way to remind myself to use my **PANDY** tools, so I made up the **Memory Jogger**.

Here's what you do. First, write down the date. Next, write down the mousework you have to do. You might write, "Color in a **PANDY Coloring Sheet** every time I feel sad." Next, look at **Memory Jogger** every day to see if there is mousework to do. Now, you are being a **Memory Jogger**.

Memory Jogger

(Sample)

PANDY SAYS

Jot down your mousework to jog your memory.

DATE: Nov. 2

MOUSEWORK: Do 5 coloring sheets when I feel worried.

DATE: Nov 9

MOUSEWORK: Do Permanent or Temporary. Do Bubble Up Your Fear worksheet each time I feel scared.

DATE: Nov 16

MOUSEWORK: Do Changing Your Tune each time I feel worried.

DATE: _____

MOUSEWORK: _____

DATE: _____

MOUSEWORK: _____

_____

_____

DATE: _____

MOUSEWORK: _____

_____

_____

DATE: _____

MOUSEWORK: _____

_____

_____

DATE: _____

MOUSEWORK: _____

_____

_____

DATE: _____

MOUSEWORK: _____

_____

_____

Memory Jogger

PANDY SAYS

Jot down your mousework to jog your memory.

DATE: _____

MOUSEWORK: _____

_____

_____

DATE: _____

MOUSEWORK: _____

_____

_____

DATE: _____

MOUSEWORK: _____

_____

_____

DATE: _____

MOUSEWORK: _____

_____

_____

DATE: _____

MOUSEWORK: _____

_____

_____

DATE: _____

MOUSEWORK: _____

_____

_____

DATE: _____

MOUSEWORK: _____

_____

_____

DATE: _____

MOUSEWORK: _____

_____

_____

DATE: _____

MOUSEWORK: _____

_____

_____

My Mouse Traps and PANDY Fix-It

GUIDELINES FOR THERAPISTS

Problem-solving is an important skill in cognitive-behavioral coping skills training (D'Zurilla, 1986; Spivack, Platt, & Shure, 1976). **My Mouse Traps** and **PANDY Fix-It** worksheets are exercises to both help children specify their problems and develop problem-solving strategies. The **My Mouse Traps** skill teaches children to identify their behavioral, cognitive, and emotional problems. The **PANDY Fix-It Worksheet** is designed to facilitate children's generation of alternative problem-solving strategies. Like most other exercises in this workbook, **My Mouse Traps** and **PANDY Fix-It** worksheets make use of metaphors and playful augmentations. Children are provided sample **My Mouse Traps** and **PANDY Fix-It** worksheets. The skill set also includes "Tips for Children."

The problem-solving skill begins with *problem identification*. Specificity is important in this first problem-solving stage. In most instances, therapists will need to shape children's problem description. The sample completed worksheet provides a good model for specificity. The following table illustrates the difference between vague and specific problem definitions.

VAGUE	SPECIFIC
Things I do that trap me (Behavioral).	**Things I do that trap me (Behavioral).**
Getting into trouble.	Hitting my sister.
Doing bad at school.	Talking to my friend when my teacher is telling us how to do homework.
Things I say to myself (Cognitive).	**Things I say to myself (Cognitive).**
"School is hard."	"I'm stupid."
"I'm not trying hard enough."	"My teachers are jerks."
"I can't handle this."	"My parents don't love me."
	"Something bad is going to happen to me."
Things I feel that trap me (Emotional).	**Things I feel that trap me (Emotional).**
Bad, psycho, squirmy	Mad, scared, worried, sad, upset, weird, pissed-off

Once the children have identified the problems in **My Mouse Traps Worksheet**, therapists are ready to make the transition to problem-solving. The problem-solving phase may be set up by several bridging questions (R. D. Friedberg, Mason, & Fidaleo, 1992). After reviewing the **My Mouse Traps Worksheet**, therapists may consider asking:

- "Which of these problems are easiest to fix?"
- "What makes them easier to fix?"
- "Which of these traps are hardest to fix?"

- "What makes them harder to fix?"
- "Which traps should we work on together first?"

Augmenting the worksheet with an animated discussion of **My Mouse Traps** may engage children in the task. Children could be asked to imitate the noise a *Mouse Trap* makes when it slaps shut. Therapists might ask children what they think it would be like to get caught in a trap. After the children have discussed these issues, therapists can guide them toward applying these concepts to their own problems. For instance, therapists might ask the youngsters:

- "What does it feel like to get stuck in your traps?"
- "What happens when you get stuck in a trap?"

After children identify their problems or mouse traps, they are ready to move on to problem-solving.

The **PANDY Fix-It** skill set includes the "Tips for Children," a sample completed **PANDY Fix-It Worksheet**, and the basic **PANDY Fix-It Worksheet**. The "Tips for Children" introduces the skill and the *Light Bulb* metaphor. *Light Bulbs* represent the different ideas children can create to solve the problem.

Problem-solving can be a relatively dry and abstract process for children. Therefore, a playful attitude toward the task is recommended. For instance, whenever a child comes up with a new idea for solving a problem, the therapist might have the child ring a bell, hit a cymbal, toot a horn, or simply yell, "Bing, Bing," to signify a new solution. These sound effects can create a conceptual anchor point for the children.

There are four basic steps on the **PANDY Fix-It Worksheet**. In step one, children note the problem on which they are planning to work. This is a relatively straightforward task and simply involves transferring one of the traps listed on the **My Mouse Traps Worksheet** to the **PANDY Fix-It Worksheet**. In step two, children are asked to come up with as many ways as they can think of to fix the problem. This phase represents the brainstorming stage. Therefore, evaluating the strategy is not necessary at this point. In fact, evaluating the options prematurely may truncate children's problem-solving process causing them to fear criticism and emit only socially desirable responses.

The next two questions emphasize evaluation. Children examine the lists of options they have created and they decide which solutions may work. Therapists and parents can help the children figure which "light bulbs" are likely to burn out. In particular, children's specific reasons for each strategy working or not working should be articulated. Learning the details associated with each option will help therapists trouble-shoot faulty or incomplete reasoning. Therapists may consider asking children:

- "What makes you guess these ways to fix the problem may not work?"
- "What does 'not working' mean?"
- "How do you know if your ways to fix the problem will not work?"
- "What are some good things that might happen if you tried your fix-it ideas?"
- "What are some bad things that might happen if you tried your fix-it ideas?"
- "How long would these fix-it ideas work?"
- "Which of these fix-it ideas would burn out?"
- "What would make the fix-it idea burn out?"

After the children evaluate their options, therapists and parents should help the youngsters implement their problem-solving ideas. It is important that parents and children are "on the same page." In this way, parents may reinforce children's efforts and provide the context for productive experimentation. Additionally, parents and children working collaboratively on a mutual problem-solving task is a robust project. Parents need to be instructed to reinforce children's adaptive problem-solving efforts. Moreover, children should be coached to deliver self-rewards for problem-solving.

After the children experiment with their newfound options, they must consider the effects the ideas produced. Children and parents should monitor whether or not their ideas worked. If their strategies were successful, children could be encouraged to continue to use them. If, on the other hand, their strategies were unsuccessful, children should be taught to evaluate why their plan did not work and prompted to develop an alternate strategy.

My Mouse Traps and PANDY Fix-It

Tips for Children

PANDY SAYS

Hi, kids. It's me, **PANDY**! These worksheets help you find ideas to solve your problems and help you prevent them. This is a two-part activity. The first part of the activity, **My Mouse Traps Worksheet**, helps you recognize your problems. The second part, **PANDY Fix-It Worksheet**, helps you solve your problems.

In **My Mouse Traps**, you list behaviors that you do or say that get you into trouble. For example, sometimes I worry a lot that I will get bad grades in school. Then, you list the things you say to yourself that <u>trap</u> and upset you. The worrying upsets me and then I say to myself, "If I get bad grades, my parents will be mad at me and I'll feel really bad." Finally, you list the things you feel that <u>trap</u> you. After I think that I'll get bad grades, I feel scared and worried.

In the **PANDY Fix-It Worksheet**, you list a problem from the **My Mouse Traps Worksheet** and think of all the possible ways you can to <u>fix it</u>. Next, you decide which of these possible ways might not work. Then, you list the best ways to solve your problem.

Of course, your counselor and parents can help you with this activity. Have fun fixing it!

My Mouse Traps Worksheet

(Sample)

Things I DO that TRAP me:

I daydream at school.
I don't write down my homework.
I don't ask other Kids to play.

Things I SAY TO MYSELF that TRAP me:

I'm not good enough.
I'll never do well in math.
Kids don't like me.

Things I FEEL that TRAP me:

Sad
Angry
Scared
Mad
Worried
Bummed - out

My Mouse Traps Worksheet

Things I DO that TRAP me:

_____

_____

_____

_____

_____

_____

Things I SAY TO MYSELF that TRAP me:

_____

_____

_____

_____

_____

_____

Things I FEEL that TRAP me:

_____

_____

_____

_____

_____

_____

PANDY Fix-It Worksheet

(Sample)

My problem is:

I don't ask kids to play.

Some ways to fix the problem are:

I could call kids up on the phone.
I could ask kids what their name is.
I could say hi to 2 kids everyday.
I could tell kids my name.
I could join in with them at recess.
I could walk home with a few kids from class.
I could go over to their house when they ask me to play.

Some ways to fix the problem that might not work are:

Joining them at recess
Calling them on the phone

Some ways to fix the problem that might work are:

Saying hi to 2 kids
Telling them my name
Going over to their house to play

PANDY Fix-It Worksheet

My problem is:

_____

_____

Some ways to fix the problem are:

_____

_____

_____

_____

_____

_____

Some ways to fix the problem that might not work are:

_____

_____

_____

_____

Some ways to fix the problem that might work are:

_____

_____

_____

_____

Bubble Up Your Fear

GUIDELINES FOR THERAPISTS

Bubble Up Your Fear is a self-monitoring task which requires children to list their fears in descending order of emotional intensity. Recording Subjective Units of Distress (SUDS) is a common practice in cognitive-behavioral therapy (Masters et al., 1987; Spiegler & Guevremont, 1998). **Bubble Up Your Fear** is a downward extension of this traditional SUDS procedure.

The **Bubble Up Your Fear Worksheet** is presented in two phases or modules. In the first phase, the children simply list, as specifically as possible, the circumstances that frighten or scare them. In phase two, they rate the intensity of the fears by coloring in the bubbles. Based on this estimate of subjective distress, the fears can be hierarchically ordered. Therapists are well-advised to gather specific information about the fears. For example, a child might list going to a birthday party as a primary fear. Therapists should try to get as much information about this fear as possible. For example, the therapist might ask:

- "What makes this scary?"
- "Does it get worse if you don't know many people at the party?"

When children rate their fears, therapists may ask, "What makes going to a party scarier than raising your hand in class?"

The bubbles metaphor serves several purposes. First, bubbles are more familiar to children than either the term Subjective Units of Distress or its acronym (SUDS). Secondly, bubbles are included on the worksheet to represent fear intensity. Children color in the number of bubbles that correspond to each fear. The more bubbles associated with the fear that are colored in, the scarier the item. Coloring in the bubbles is a fun and concrete way to rate fears. Thirdly, bubbles provide a useful therapeutic metaphor for scared feelings. Like bubbles, scared feelings are temporary phenomena that last for a while and then dissipate.

Children seem to respond very well to the bubbles metaphor. Children could be given bottles of toy bubbles that are found in many toy stores. As children complete their worksheet, they can be encouraged to blow bubbles. Connecting the concrete act of playing with bubbles and the abstract process of rating subjective distress may promote greater recall. Moreover, therapists can use the real bubbles as an experiential exercise to teach children about the transient nature of anxiety.

As they blow bubbles, children may be asked to observe what happens to the bubbles. They are instructed to watch the bubbles form, float through the air, last a while, and then burst. Therapists may then draw the analogy between bubbles and scared feelings. The following confabulated transcript* illustrates the process.

Therapist:	You boys and girls are experts at blowing bubbles. Let's watch the bubbles for a little bit. What do you see happening?
Susie:	They float away.
John:	They stick on your finger.
Eric:	They make a mess.
Julie:	Some are big and some are little.

---

*Names and identifying information have been disguised throughout this workbook to protect confidentiality.

Therapist:	Wow, we really saw a lot. Some float away, some stick, some are messy, some are big, and some are little. Do some last longer than others?
John:	Yes.
Therapist:	What causes some bubbles to last longer than others?
Susie:	Well, we burst some of them and popped some of them.
Eric:	Some landed on a different surface.
Therapist:	Hmm. So there are things we can do to make the bubbles last longer and not so long?
Children:	Yeah!
Therapist:	Now, let me see. How are the bubbles like the fears we just talked about? Are some bigger than others?
Susie:	Yes, my fear of parties is bigger than my fear of dogs.
Therapist:	Do you think there are things you could do to make your scared feelings last longer and not so long?

The **Bubble Up Your Fears Worksheet** concludes with an example of a coping statement that children write on an index card: *"Your scared feelings are just like bubbles. They are there for awhile and then they float away."* This coping card is an initial way to help children who believe their anxiety is interminable realize anxiety has a natural waxing and waning course. Children can be instructed to keep the card with them and review it when they become anxious. Finally, the coping statement could form a hypothesis for subsequent behavioral experiments. For example, "Let's see if we can figure out whether this statement is true for you. How can we test it out?"

Bubble Up Your Fear begins with the identification of fears or worries. After listing the fears, the child rates their level of fear by coloring in bubbles to represent how scared he/she is. Next, the youngster ranks the fears from most to least scary. In the final section, the child learns that scared feelings are temporary. After identifying and quantifying their fears, the child is prepared to challenge their fears.

Bubble Up Your Fear

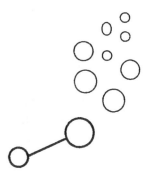

Tips for Children

PANDY SAYS

Hi, boys and girls. I love to blow bubbles. I like the way bubbles form and then they float away. Sometimes I like to burst the bubbles. Do you like to do any of these things?

Bubbles kind of remind me of fears and worries. They float around you and then they go away. I made up a worksheet that is called **Bubble Up Your Fear**. I hope it helps you quiet down your worries and fears.

First, write down your worries and fears. Start with the fears and worries that upset you the most. Next, color in the bubbles to show how strong your fears or worries are. For example, for your strongest fear, color in 10 bubbles, for the next, color in 9 bubbles, for the next, color 8, and so on. Tell your counselor or therapist why each fear or worry is worth the number of bubbles you colored in. Lastly, write down my note that says: ***"Your scared feelings are just like bubbles. They are there for awhile and then they float away."*** Read over the card whenever you feel scared.

Bubble Up Your Fear Worksheet

(Sample)

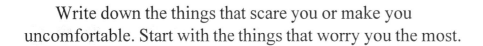

PANDY SAYS

Write down the things that scare you or make you uncomfortable. Start with the things that worry you the most.

1. Go over to a friend's to play.
2. Inviting a friend to come over to my house.
3. Having a friend come over to my house.
4. Getting invited to a friend's house.
5. Eating a snack over at my friend's house.
6. Finding someone to play with at recess.
7. _____
8. _____
9. _____
10. _____

Write a reminder of the fear from the previous page next to each number. Now color in the number of bubbles that go with each fear.

1. Going to friends to play ●●●●●●●●●○

2. Inviting friend to my house ●●●●●●●●○○

3. Having friend at my house ●●●●●●○○○

4. Getting invited to friends ●●●●●○○○○

5. Eating snacks at friends ●●●●○○○○○

6. Finding someone to play with at recess ●●●●○○○○○○

7. _____ ○○○○○○○○○

8. _____ ○○○○○○○○○

9. _____ ○○○○○○○○○

10. _____ ○○○○○○○○○

PANDY SAYS

Remember your scared feelings are just like bubbles. They are there for awhile and then they float away.

Bubble Up Your Fear Worksheet

PANDY SAYS

Write down the things that scare you or make you
uncomfortable. Start with the things that worry you the most.

1. _____

2. _____

3. _____

4. _____

5. _____

6. _____

7. _____

8. _____

9. _____

10. _____

Write a reminder of the fear from the previous page next to each number. Now color in the number of bubbles that go with each fear.

1. _____ ○ ○ ○ ○ ○ ○ ○ ○ ○ ○

2. _____ ○ ○ ○ ○ ○ ○ ○ ○ ○ ○

3. _____ ○ ○ ○ ○ ○ ○ ○ ○ ○ ○

4. _____ ○ ○ ○ ○ ○ ○ ○ ○ ○ ○

5. _____ ○ ○ ○ ○ ○ ○ ○ ○ ○ ○

6. _____ ○ ○ ○ ○ ○ ○ ○ ○ ○ ○

7. _____ ○ ○ ○ ○ ○ ○ ○ ○ ○ ○

8. _____ ○ ○ ○ ○ ○ ○ ○ ○ ○ ○

9. _____ ○ ○ ○ ○ ○ ○ ○ ○ ○ ○

10. _____ ○ ○ ○ ○ ○ ○ ○ ○ ○ ○

PANDY SAYS

Remember your scared feelings are just like bubbles. They are there for awhile and then they float away.

Catching Feelings and Thoughts

GUIDELINES FOR THERAPISTS

The **Catching Feelings and Thoughts Diary** is a self-monitoring task that includes a graduated thought diary or thought record. The Automatic Thought Record (ATR) is a common cognitive-behavioral technique. The most frequently used thought record is a five-column diary developed by Beck et al. (1979). In the five-column record, clients are typically asked to report the situation, feelings, and thoughts in the first three columns. Additionally, they construct an alternative thought in column four and rerate their mood in column five. Often, this is a daunting task for adults, let alone for a 9-year-old child. Accordingly, simplification of thought records has been recommended by various authors (J. S. Beck, 1995; R. D. Friedberg et al., 1999).

There are several examples of developmentally sensitive thought records in the literature (Kendall et al., 1992; Seligman et al., 1995). Each of these thought records includes a thought bubble where children can write their thoughts. Wellman, Hollander, and Schult (1996) found that even very young children understand thought bubbles.

The **Catching Feelings and Thoughts Diary** is unique in several ways. It sets up other thought testing techniques such as **Clue Snooping** and **Thought Digger**. Secondly, the **Catching Feelings and Thoughts Diary** calls for children to draw a feeling face on the familiar PANDY cartoon and then write the feeling word label (e.g., mad) above the cartoon. As readers may recall, this is an identical task to the one described in the **PANDY Coloring Sheets**. Thus, the task of completing a thought record is simplified by the fact that the children already are familiar and practiced with skills identifying and reporting feelings.

The **Catching Feelings and Thoughts Diary** requires the children to rate the intensity of their feelings. It is quite common for children to describe their feelings in all-or-none terms. Rating their level of feeling is a novel task for youngsters. The traffic signal is a familiar icon to children and simply communicates the notions of varying levels of emotional intensity. Children readily understand that *red* signals the highest level of intensity, *yellow* represents moderate intensity, and *green* reflects low intensity.

Levels of feeling intensity can be rated on various scales. For instance, on a traditional ATR used with adults, emotions are rated on a 1 to 100 scale (A. T. Beck et al., 1979). Many cognitive therapists commonly ask patients to rate their feelings on a 1 to 10 scale. We elected to use a shorter scale range to promote children's compliance and understanding. Having to choose between three levels of feeling by simply coloring in the appropriate "bulb" on the traffic light is a simpler task than estimating their feeling level on an abstract scale ranging from 1 to 10.

Next, children record their thoughts in the thought bubble column. Many therapists often complain that they have difficulty eliciting psychologically meaningful automatic thoughts. Therapists are well-advised to ask children, *"What is going through your mind right now?"* rather than asking children, "What are your thoughts?" or "What were you thinking?" (J. S. Beck, 1995; Padeskey & Greenberger, 1995). Clinical experience shows that these latter two questions produce intellectualized, emotionally sanitized cognitive products. Accordingly, therapists should attempt to ask "What's going through your mind right now?" or any variant such as:

- "What popped into your mind?"
- "What flew into your mind?"
- "What zipped into your mind?"
- "What did you tell yourself?"
- "What did you say to yourself?"

Children are also supplied with several sample thought diaries. These sample thought records show completed **Catching Feelings and Thoughts** diaries. Each example is written in a child's handwriting. Finally, there are separate sample thought diaries for anxious, sad, and angry feelings.

Having fun with the **Catching Feelings and Thoughts Diary** adds to the reinforcement value. For example, therapists may play catch with the child while they identify their feelings and thoughts. Playing catch in session may be a memorable experience and furnish the child with a concrete conceptual anchor upon which to base the information. Therapists could play catch and use the well-practiced act of catching as an example of an automatic process (R. D. Friedberg, 1993).

Therapists and children could play with the *traffic signal icon*. They might invent active games associated with the **Catching Feelings and Thoughts Diary**. For instance, children could play a version of "Red Light, Green Light" with the therapist. Therapists could then talk about how a red light feeling keeps you stuck in place whereas green light feelings allow you to go forward. Therapists could then have the children walk during GREEN LIGHT instructions and stop in place at the RED LIGHT command. At the RED LIGHT point, the therapist could give a situation, such as, "Someone calls you a name." Next the child is asked, "What goes through your mind?" This is an active and fun way to teach identifying thoughts and feelings. This is another way to engage the children and solidify their understanding of the skills.

This exercise is an entertaining approach for teaching a core skill. After briefly stating the event, the child draws a mouth on PANDY, colors in the feeling signal, and writes down the negative thoughts. The **Catching Feelings and Thoughts Diary** teaches children to identify thoughts, feelings, and events in a playful manner. Finally, the "catching" metaphor could be a springboard for a variety of other therapeutic activities.

Catching Feelings and Thoughts

Tips for Children

PANDY SAYS

Hi, kids. It's me, **PANDY**! I like baseball. Do you like to catch a ball? Think about what you have to do to catch a ball. You have to watch it and then put your hands up to catch it. It's kind of the same thing when you catch thoughts. First, you have to pay attention to them and then you ask yourself, "What's going through my mind?"

The **Catching Feelings and Thoughts Diary** helps you capture the thoughts and feelings you have about your problem. First, you write down the event that's troubling you. Next draw the mouth on me, **PANDY**, to show how you feel. Write the name of the feeling over my picture. Then color in how strong your feeling is. For example, red means a lot, yellow in the middle, and green not too much. Next, write down what's going through your mind in the thought bubble. Finally, write down the date that you completed the diary. Look at the sample diaries for examples and ask your counselor or parents for help.

Catching Feelings and Thoughts Diary

(Sample)

EVENT (what happened): _Susan and Bobby made fun of_

_me._

PANDY'S FEELING:	PANDY'S FEELING SIGNAL	PANDY'S THOUGHT BUBBLE

PANDY'S FEELING: Sad

PANDY'S FEELING SIGNAL

RED

YELLOW

GREEN

PANDY'S THOUGHT BUBBLE

I must be weird if these kids are teasing me.

PANDY

Date: Jan. 23

Catching Feelings and Thoughts Diary

(Sample)

EVENT (what happened): <u>Going to school in the morning</u>

PANDY'S
FEELING:

<u>anxious</u>

PANDY'S
FEELING
SIGNAL

PANDY'S
THOUGHT
BUBBLE

RED

YELLOW

GREEN

PANDY

I will miss my mommy so much I will not be able to stand it.

Date:

Dec. 6

Catching Feelings and Thoughts Diary

(Sample)

EVENT (what happened): I was playing with my friends and they did not do what I wanted to do.

| PANDY'S FEELING: | PANDY'S FEELING SIGNAL | PANDY'S THOUGHT BUBBLE |

Angry

Date:
Jan. 29

Catching Feelings and Thoughts Diary

EVENT (what happened): _____

_____

_____

| PANDY'S FEELING: | PANDY'S FEELING SIGNAL | PANDY'S THOUGHT BUBBLE |

_____

RED

YELLOW

GREEN

Date:

Priming
Exercises

Permanent or Temporary

GUIDELINES FOR THERAPISTS

The next exercises and activities are priming techniques focused on helping children become more flexible in their thinking. Distressed children often become rigid problem-solvers and are unable to adopt multiple perspectives on their problems. More specifically, depressed children tend to confuse *permanent* and *temporary* causes (Jaycox et al., 1994; Nolen-Hoeksema & Girgus, 1995; Nolen-Hoeksema, Girgus, & Seligman, 1996; Seligman et al., 1995). Simply, they tend to attribute negative outcomes to more stable, enduring causes. This type of explanatory style promotes pessimism and hopelessness. Accordingly, helping children see that most situations and feelings are more temporary than permanent can create a window of opportunity for counselors and therapists. When children see the possibility of change, they are likely to become more motivated for change to occur.

Priming techniques are activities or processes that grease the wheels of change (Riskind, 1991; Riskind, Sarampote, & Mercier, 1996). Generally, we recommend that you use the priming exercises prior to the cognitive techniques such as **Me/Not Me, Catching Feelings and Thoughts, Breaking the Crystal Ball, Clue Snooping,** and so forth. The priming exercises prepare the child for the more advanced cognitive material. Moreover, the priming techniques are graduated tasks and allow the child a sense of mastery before having to attempt the more difficult tasks. Lastly, these priming tasks can stimulate discussions and get children talking with therapists about nonthreatening topics. Using the **Permanent or Temporary Worksheet** is nonjudgmental and exploratory rather than interrogative in nature. More specifically, we encourage therapists to ask discussion questions such as:

- "What makes _____ seem permanent to you?"
- "How can you tell whether something is permanent or temporary?"

The important point to remember is there are no "correct" responses to the worksheet. In this worksheet, children's responses are simply data to be worked with rather than answers to be graded. Certainly, devoting session time to communicating the notion that there are no right answers is time well spent.

After the items have been circled, the therapist should ask the child to count the number of circles in each column. While there are likely to be individual differences in items, overall there should be more circles in the temporary column. The therapist can then process this "data" with suggested key questions such as:

- "Which column has more circles?"
- "What do you suppose that means?"
- "Did you expect that there would be more permanent or temporary things?"
- "When you look at the list on the worksheet, which things will we be working on together?"
- "Of these things, how many are changeable, and how many are unchangeable?"
- "If more things are changeable, what does that mean about the things we are working on?"
- "When you look at the list on the worksheet, which of the things are you most in charge of?"
- "Of these things, how many are changeable and how many are unchangeable?"
- "If more things are changeable, what does that mean about you being in charge of your thoughts, feelings, and behaviors?"

After the child constructs an adaptive response or conclusion based on completion of the worksheet, therapists and counselors should encourage the child *to write these responses on an index card*. For instance, the child might write, *"My thoughts and feelings are changeable"* on an index card. By writing these responses on cards, children have a ready, self-instructional coping statement to use when they see problems as potentially insurmountable. The cards make the task more portable and applicable to various circumstances. Finally, children are encouraged to write the question, *"Am I confusing Permanent and Temporary?"* on an index card. Teaching youngsters to ask themselves this question when they feel distressed is a gainful therapeutic strategy.

The concept of *permanent versus temporary* is a crucial premise in teaching a child to change. Once the youngster understands that many feelings are *temporary*, he or she gains a feeling of control. This self-efficacy is a precursor to handling the unpleasant feeling and developing a plan for change. The priming task is a simple first step paving the way for progress.

Permanent or Temporary

Tips for Children

PANDY SAYS

Do you ever get confused about whether some things will change or if they will stay the same? It is important to understand whether things are permanent or temporary. Permanent means something stays the same forever, like your eye color. Temporary means it will change, like your feelings. Do you know why this is important? When you believe something is permanent, like a sad feeling, and it is really temporary, you tend to feel hopeless and unable to change things. If you believe something is temporary, but it's not and it's really permanent, you might feel frustrated when you cannot change it. So, it's important to figure out if things that bother you are permanent or temporary so you can know what you can change and what you cannot change.

The next worksheet, **Permanent or Temporary**, is an activity aimed at trying to help learn more about permanent and temporary things. Filling it out will help you feel more in charge. Work with your counselor and have fun talking about what makes things permanent or temporary.

Permanent or Temporary Worksheet

Circle whether these things are <u>temporary</u> (will change) or <u>permanent</u> (won't change)

The weather	Temporary (changes)	Permanent (does not change)
Your thoughts	Temporary (changes)	Permanent (does not change)
Your feelings	Temporary (changes)	Permanent (does not change)
How hard school is for you	Temporary (changes)	Permanent (does not change)
Who your relatives are	Temporary (changes)	Permanent (does not change)
When someone dies	Temporary (changes)	Permanent (does not change)
How bored you are	Temporary (changes)	Permanent (does not change)
The things that scare you	Temporary (changes)	Permanent (does not change)
Your hairstyle	Temporary (changes)	Permanent (does not change)
Your fingerprints	Temporary (changes)	Permanent (does not change)
How hungry or thirsty you are	Temporary (changes)	Permanent (does not change)
The number of pages in a book	Temporary (changes)	Permanent (does not change)

Sticks and Stones

GUIDELINES FOR THERAPISTS

The **Sticks and Stones Worksheet** is another priming technique (Riskind, 1991; Riskind et al., 1996) used to increase cognitive flexibility and teach children about "All or None Labels" (A. T. Beck et al., 1979; J. S. Beck, 1995; Burns, 1980). The worksheet is relatively simple to complete, requiring the child to read an item, decide whether it is a *Sticks and Stones Label*, and then put a **Big X** through the *Sticks and Stones Labels*. Similarly to the other priming techniques in the workbook, we recommend that they be used to set up the complex tasks such as **Clue Snooping, Thought Digger, Changing Your Tune**, and so on.

The child should read the definition of *Sticks and Stones Labels* provided on the worksheet. After reading the definition, therapists might ask key processing questions such as:

- "What part don't you understand?"
- "What part do you understand?"
- "Can you give an example of a *Sticks and Stones Label* you sometimes say to yourself?"

Therapists should work to clarify any misunderstandings. Once the therapist is confident that the child understands the concept, the child can begin the exercise. The child reads the item and decides whether it is a *Sticks and Stones Label*. The therapeutic goal is for the child to internalize the process of identifying maladaptive and self-denigrating labels, learn to question themselves, and then discard inaccurate, distressing, self-recriminations. As a way to promote this process, the therapist may encourage children to write down the question, "*Am I calling myself a Sticks and Stones Label?*" on an index card. Careful attention should be paid to the children's responses. If a therapist notices that a youngster inaccurately identifies a *Sticks and Stones Label*, they should discuss the item with the child. The therapist might query, "What makes this seem like a *Sticks and Stones Label* to you?"

After the therapist is confident that the child understands the concept, efforts are directed at applying the concept to the child's life experiences. Sample questions might be:

- "What *Sticks and Stones Labels* do you call yourself?"
- "How do you feel when you call yourself the label?"

When the child identifies the *Sticks and Stones Label*, it should be written down on a piece of paper. Once the label is written on paper, the therapist should encourage the child to animatedly **DISCARD** the label. The label could be crumpled, ripped, cut into small pieces with scissors, or stomped on. Finally, the child *throws the label into the trash can*. Therapists are encouraged to play up the dramatic discarding of the label. The action reminds the children to *recognize the "trash-talking"* internal dialogue, pull it out of his or her mind, and *dump* it in the garbage.

After the child has dumped the label in the trash, the therapist can spend some time processing the experience. For example, the therapist might ask, "What was it like for you to throw away your label?" Therapists can then specifically connect the abstract metaphor to a more concrete action, which the child can perform. The therapist might ask, "When *Sticks and Stones Labels* go through your mind, how can you throw them away?" Children can be encouraged to write a question to help them recognize and handle the negative self-talk on an index card. A sample reminder to write on an index card could include, "*Is this a Sticks and Stones Label?*" They can pull out their card whenever they have a distressing feeling to help them recognize if they are bashing themselves. After the child recognizes the negative things he or she says to himself/herself, it is easier to attempt to replace the negative labels with more accurate statements.

The **Sticks and Stones** exercise trains the child to recognize and minimize self-denigrating name-calling. By recognizing negative self-talk and "put-downs," the youngster can learn to stop the name-calling. The **Sticks and Stones** skill is an action-packed nonthreatening way for children to identify and modify their self-criticisms. Through this exercise, children gain an introduction to cognitive skills and are prepared for more advanced techniques requiring self-instruction and rational analysis.

Sticks and Stones

Tips for Children

PANDY SAYS

Do you ever watch sports on TV? Have you ever heard of "trash-talking"? Trash-talking is when one player calls another player a name. ***Sticks and Stones Labels*** are names you call yourself that make you feel badly about yourself.

These ***Sticks and Stones Labels*** are really useless. Instead of helping you, these labels tell you things you can't or won't change. Some examples of ***Sticks and Stones Labels*** are, "I'm a jerk, I'm a loser, I'm stupid, I'm ugly, I'm no good." The more you use these ***Sticks and Stones Labels*** on yourself, the more they will stick with you like a piece of old bubble gum on the bottom of your shoe.

I want you to learn to get rid of these <u>useless</u> ***Sticks and Stones Labels*** and stop talking trash to yourself. Try out my **Sticks and Stones Worksheet** for practice.

Sticks and Stones Worksheet

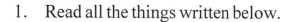

PANDY SAYS

1. Read all the things written below.

2. Remember a **<u>Sticks and Stones Label</u>** is a name you call yourself that makes you feel badly about yourself. They are useless things because they do not tell you what you can do differently. They are ways that you talk trash to yourself.

3. Decide whether the statements below are **<u>Sticks and Stones Labels</u>** or not.

4. Put a BIG X through the **<u>Sticks and Stones Labels</u>** with a crayon or marker.

"I'm a bully."

"I'm stupid."

"I'm ugly."

"I'm bad."

"I forget how to spell some words at school."

"I don't do what I am told sometimes."

"I get angry."

"I don't like cleaning my room."

"Sometimes I don't listen well."

"I'm a girl."

"Some math problems are hard for me."

"I play soccer."

"I get sad."

"I am a boy."

"I get scared."

"I like Barbies."

EXERCISE 10
Many Meanings

GUIDELINES FOR THERAPISTS

The **Many Meanings Worksheet** is a priming exercise that includes simple directions for the child, a sample item, and six exercises for the child to complete. The goal of the **Many Meanings Worksheet** is to increase the child's consideration of multiple perspectives and prepare the child for reattribution techniques.

Reattribution is a standard cognitive-behavioral technique (A. T. Beck et al., 1979; J. S. Beck, 1995). When children are distressed, their information processing becomes overly truncated and the children become fixated on one explanation for the situation or stressor. This narrow perspective creates a type of "tunnel vision" where competing possibilities are neglected. When discussing depressed individuals, A.T. Beck (1985) has referred to this restricted range of thinking as the "cognitive blockade" (p. 336). A cognitive blockade preempts the attributional search process and reattribution procedures prompt continued exploration for new explanations. Reattribution procedures are aimed at attenuating the blockade and expanding children's realization of multiple perspectives.

The **Many Meanings Worksheet** may be helpful in the initial stages of therapy with depressed children who automatically gravitate to one particular explanation for their stressors. The **Many Meanings Worksheet** does not require the child to come up with a stressful situation. Rather, the situations are provided for them. Further, the child does not have to report their own cognitions. Thus, it is a graduated priming task where the child learns to think flexibly about typical situations, but it does not demand reporting problematic events or cognitions. Accordingly, **Many Meanings** may be used to prepare the child for more sophisticated tasks such as **Changing Your Tune, Catching Feelings and Thoughts, Thought Digger, Clue Snooping, Breaking the Crystal Ball, Surf the Angry Sea,** and **Tease Whiz.**

Inviting the child to read the first paragraph under PANDY SAYS is a useful way to introduce the worksheet. After the child has read the paragraph, counselors and therapists can ask several processing questions such as:

- "Do you ever think there is only one meaning for the things that bother you?"
- "What problems are caused by thinking of only one meaning?"
- "How does thinking there is only one meaning cause problems for you?"
- "How might thinking up many meanings help you?"
- "Are you willing to try out ways to come up with **Many Meanings**?"

An example is provided below the PANDY SAYS text. The child should read the example and ask, *"What else could this mean?"* to seek alternate meanings. Checking with the child and asking several processing questions are good therapeutic strategies. Key processing questions might include:

- "How does thinking that 'funny stomach noises mean something bad will happen,' make PANDY feel?"
- "How would coming up with **Many Meanings** for stomach noises help?"
- "What other meanings could you come up with?"
- "What parts of this make sense to you?"
- "What parts do not make sense?"

There are six items on the worksheet that represent common situations and accompanying beliefs. Therapists should select items that are similar to the child's presenting problems. As the child reads the item aloud, the therapist can cue the child with the question, *"What else could this mean?"* After the child constructs an alternative meaning, the therapist may ask:

- "How much do you believe this?"
- "How does believing this make you feel?"

The remaining situations may be assigned for homework. Additionally, the therapist should invite the child to write the question, *"What else could this mean?"* on an index card. Therapists can then instruct the children to keep their card with them and ask themselves, *"What else could this mean?"* whenever they are in distressing situations in which they narrowly construe possibilities.

The **Many Meanings Worksheet** guides children in finding alternative possibilities for their negative thoughts. If a child learns to be more flexible in his or her thinking, the negative thoughts become less powerful. By habitually asking, *"What else could this mean?"* the self-questioning process can become automatic. Ultimately, children can direct their attention to both the external and internal causes for negative events.

Many Meanings

Tips for Children

PANDY SAYS

Hello, boys and girls. You know that the way we explain things shapes how we feel and what we do. We all try to understand the things that bother us. When we try to understand the reasons things happen we ask ourselves, "*What does this mean?*" The way we answer this question helps us make sense of the world around us.

When I get upset, I think there is only one way to understand the things that trouble me. I think that the worst will happen, that things will never change, or people will not like me. I am thinking that there is only one meaning when there are **Many Meanings**.

I made up this worksheet so I could get practice coming up with **Many Meanings**. I wrote down six things that could bother you and you have to figure out why these events occurred. I want you to ask yourself the question, "*What else could this mean?*" and see if you come up with **Many Meanings.**

After you finish the worksheet, write down the question, "*What else could this mean?*" on an index card. Keep the card with you. When you get upset about something and you think there is only one way to explain it, ask yourself, "*What else could this mean?*" See how many meanings you can come up with.

If you have any questions, talk it over with your counselor and parents.

Many Meanings Worksheet

PANDY SAYS

I wrote about some things that bother me. I thought there was only one meaning for all these things, but **I WAS WRONG**. There can be many meanings. See if you can think of two more meanings for each of the things that bother me. If you get stuck, look at my example:

EXAMPLE:

My stomach is making funny noises. This means something bad will happen. **WHAT ELSE COULD THIS MEAN?**

1. I'm just upset. Being upset does not mean something bad will happen.

2. My stomach is working. It's a normal sound.

Going to a basketball team meeting where I don't know anybody means I will be left out and no one will want to play with me. **WHAT ELSE COULD THIS MEAN?**

1. _____

_____

2. _____

_____

Someone in my class is making faces at me and that means she hates me. **WHAT ELSE COULD THIS MEAN?**

1. _____

_____

2. _____

_____

Feeling scared means something bad is going to happen. **WHAT ELSE COULD THIS MEAN?**

1. _____

_____

2. _____

_____

If I do something wrong, it means I am terrible. **WHAT ELSE COULD THIS MEAN?**

1. _____

_____

2. _____

_____

Even one mistake is a bad thing. **WHAT ELSE COULD THIS MEAN?**

1. _____

   _____

2. _____

   _____

While standing in line, a child pushes me, that means I should punch him. **WHAT ELSE COULD THIS MEAN?**

1. _____

   _____

2. _____

   _____

Self-Instructional Methods

Me/Not Me

GUIDELINES FOR THERAPISTS

The **Me/Not Me Worksheet** is a self-instructional technique designed to modify children's tendency to focus on themselves as the cause of problems. This type of thinking error has been referred to as personalization (J. S. Beck, 1995; Burns, 1980). Simply, children are overemphasizing negative aspects of themselves as causes for events. The automatic nature of this information processing style contributes to children excluding other plausible explanations for the events. Personalization is often associated with such dysphoric feelings such as guilt, depression, shame, and anxiety. The **Me/Not Me Worksheet** invites children to record the problematic or stressful event and then ask themselves a set of questions. When the child records the problematic event, he or she should be coached to write the event in a specific and objective manner.

After the child has identified the event or stressor, the questioning process is initiated. The first question asks children to consider, *"What things other than ME might have caused this to happen?"* This question is offered first as a way to interrupt the automatic personalization process. Thus, the child prone to excessive self-blame must ponder all other aspects of the situation before considering their contribution to the problem.

The next step in the process is to have the child account for their own responsibility after they have considered other alternatives. This step is formalized by having the child record their responses to the question, *"What did I do to make this happen?"* Some therapists may worry that considering other alternatives before taking personal responsibility will create avoidance. However, it is important to remember that *this therapeutic task is for children who automatically accept an excessive amount of personal responsibility and engage in inordinate self-blame*. The task is not suited for children who deny or avoid personal responsibility.

Following the consideration of external causes with identification of personal causes balances children's thinking. Since the child's pattern tends toward self-blame, achieving an equilibrium becomes more likely if external causes are initially examined. However, the analysis of personal causes is also necessary to create more realistic appraisals. Children will not believe they have absolutely nothing to do with the occurrence of events. *The goal of this task is to help children more accurately discern their personal responsibility and then take charge of the things they can change for themselves.*

Accordingly, the third step in the process helps the child identify which area he or she has control over. In our experience, children respond well to the question, *"Which things are you in charge of?"* When the children gain a better sense of the details they can control, they may experience a boost in their self-efficacy.

In the final step, the children make a plan that includes a problem-solving component for the items that they can control, and an acknowledgement of the circumstances for which they have little or no responsibility. Thus, the plan is an action strategy that achieves a balance between maintaining personal responsibility and distancing oneself from events that are beyond one's control or responsibility.

Therapists and counselors are well-advised to help make the child's plan specific and achievable. Relevant details and graduated tasks ought to be included in the plan. Steps for achieving the plan should also be articulated. Therapists should take care that the details in the plan are under the child's control. The **Me/Not Me Worksheet** sample can be reviewed with the child to illuminate how each column is completed.

The **Me/Not Me** activity will teach the child to clearly articulate the upsetting event. Next, considering many other possibilities for the stressor other than himself/herself will broaden the youngster's thinking. After assuming a broader external perspective, the child returns to his or her own responsibility and control. Finally, by making an action plan, the child learns to take action to solve his or her own problems.

Me/Not Me

Tips for Children

PANDY SAYS

Many times when boys and girls feel guilty and sad, they blame themselves too much for what happens. Sometimes, they are to blame, but many times depressed boys and girls take more of their share of the blame than they deserve. They blame themselves for things that they have little or nothing to do with. It is a good idea for boys and girls to clearly figure out what they did to cause problems to happen and what things other than themselves caused problems. The **Me/Not Me Worksheet** is an exercise that may help you. Here's what you do:

1. Check out my **Me/Not Me Worksheet** sample and follow along.

2. Write down the event or the problem that you are blaming yourself for.

3. Ask yourself, "***What things, other than something about me, may have caused this to happen?***"

4. List as many things as you can think of.

5. Ask yourself, "***What might I have done to cause the problem?***"

6. Ask yourself, "***Which of these things do I have control of?***"

7. Next, <u>work out a plan</u> to take charge of the things you can control.

Me/Not Me Worksheet

(Sample)

EVENT	What things other than ME might have caused this to happen?	What did I do to make this happen?	Which things can I control?	What is my plan?
My friend has an unhappy look on her face and she has been acting crabby.	Her mom and dad yelled at her this morning. She got a bad grade in school. She lost her favorite pencil.	I didn't call her back when she called me on the phone last night.	The only thing I can control is whether I called her back or not.	I could ask her if she wants to chat. I could ask her if she wants to play after school.

Me/Not Me Worksheet

EVENT	What things other than ME might have caused this to happen?	What did I do to make this happen?	Which things can I control?	What is my plan?

Changing Your Tune

GUIDELINES FOR THERAPISTS

The **Changing Your Tune** skill package includes the "Tips for Children," **Changing Your Tune Practice Diary,** and the **Changing Your Tune Diary.** The skill package is a priming and self-instructional procedure where the child is provided with sample events, feelings, and thoughts. The child's task is to respond to the negative thought with a more positive counter-thought. In the **Changing Your Tune Diary,** the child completes the event, feeling, thought, and counter-thought columns. The **Changing Your Tune Diary** represents an opportunity for the children to apply the skills learned in the worksheet to their personal experiences.

The **Changing Your Tune** skill set is based on the self-talk and self-control models of cognitive-behavioral therapy (Kendall et al., 1992; Meichenbaum, 1985). In these models, children are instructed to replace unproductive, maladaptive self-statements with more productive coping thoughts. The **Changing Your Tune** skill set is a method for teaching children ways to replace distressing thoughts with more facilitative thoughts.

The **Changing Your Tune** skill is based on the analogy between musical songs, lyrics, and thoughts. Simply, the therapist asks children about songs that they cannot seem to get out of their head. Once they have identified the song lyrics, the therapist makes the connections between lyrics that go over and over in their mind and the negative thoughts that travel through their mind. This is a useful analogy because it teaches the children about the automatic nature of negative thoughts. Moreover, the therapist communicates via the analogy that these thoughts are learned through practice. Accordingly, since they were initially learned, they can be unlearned. Thus, the analogy is a useful tool to help the children learn they can change repetitive patterns.

The process begins with the child reading the text from "Tips for Children." After the child reads the first paragraph, the therapist can ask several key processing questions:

- "What song goes through your mind?"
- "What are the words to the song?"
- "How did it get stuck in your mind?"
- "How did you learn the words so well that they got stuck in your head?"

Next, the child and therapist move to the second paragraph. The child reads the text and the therapist continues to process the material with the child. After the child finishes the paragraph, the therapist could ask more key processing questions such as:

- "How does this sound to you?"
- "What parts do you agree with?"
- "What parts do you disagree with?"

Therapists can take this opportunity to reinforce the connection between song lyrics and the negative thoughts. For instance they could say:

"The negative things that go through your head are just like the words to the song you can't get out of your head. You've heard them over and over and just have not learned to stop listening to them.

Would you like to stop listening to the negative things that go through your head? Then, let's keep reading."

The therapist continues to invite the child to read through paragraphs two and three in the text. After the child reads the paragraphs, the therapist might ask the following processing questions:

- "What things went through PANDY's mind when no one wanted to play?"
- "How might those things make PANDY feel?"
- "Do those type of things go through your mind when no one seems to want to play with you?"
- "What other things go through your mind when you feel _____?"
- "Do you have some old tunes that go through your mind when you feel badly? Let's see what PANDY does, OK?"

The child then continues to finish the text. After completing the text material, it is recommended that therapists further process the information with the child before moving on to the worksheet. The following are some sample processing questions:

- "What did PANDY do to feel better?"
- "What happened to the old tunes?"
- "What changed them?"
- "What is the difference between the old tune and the new tunes?"
- "Do you guess that you could change your tunes?"
- "How much might it help?"
- "How much are you willing to try to change your tune?"
- "How will we know if it is working?"

The **Changing Your Tune Practice Diary** is the next step following the "Tips for Children" text. The **Changing Your Tune Practice Diary** is a graduated task that provides children with sample events, feelings, and negative automatic thoughts. The child is then asked to supply a new thought or tune that counters the negative automatic thought. The first item on the practice worksheet includes a sample new tune so the child has a model or template for completing the sheet. This practice diary is slightly different from other samples or practice items in the workbook. The child only constructs a new tune or coping response to several situations, feelings, and "old tunes." In this way, the child gains practice with self-instruction but does not have to manage heavy task demands.

The practice diary includes various situations, feelings, and accompanying thoughts. The diary includes several prototypical events, feelings, and thoughts. We recommend that therapists select items from the sheet that approximate the child's presenting symptoms. By selecting items in this way, the therapist normalizes the child's concerns and furnishes another opportunity for graduated practice. Moreover, working on items relevant to the child's problems makes the therapy more meaningful and individualizes treatment.

If the child experiences difficulty creating a new tune, the therapist should try to coach the child through the response. Effective new tunes make sense of the event, seem believable to the child, and decrease the negative feelings. For example, the following key questions and probes for Item 4 (Say goodbye to my mom and dad at school) may facilitate the coaching process:

- "What things could you say to yourself that would help you feel less worried?"
- "What might be other ways to think about saying goodbye to mom and dad?"
- "Which of these things are believable to you?"
- "Which of these things make sense to you?"
- "Which of these things would help you the most?"
- "Which of these things would you be able to say?"
- "Which of these things would help you feel less worried?"

After the child is coached to develop a coping statement (new thought/tune), the statement is recorded on the worksheet. Effective coping responses can be transferred from the worksheet to an index card in order to make the skill more portable. Thus, the children are gaining experience in developing more productive internal dialogues. These practice responses prepare them for completing their **Changing Your Tune Diary.**

In the first column in the **Changing Your Tune Diary**, the child is asked to write down a distressing and problematic event. The child can refer to the examples in the previously completed **Changing Your Tune Practice Diary**. The therapist can ask if the child had similar events or situations happen to them. The therapist should be sure to coach the child through the first few entries in the **Changing Your Tune Diary**.

It is relatively common for a child to become stuck constructing a new counter-thought. The child may come up with a rather platitudinous, simplistic response or an unbelievable "Pollyannaish" thought. In these instances, therapists need to guide the child toward more effective coping thoughts. The coping thought should directly address the stressor and supply a coping response. Ideally, *the new tune or coping response should include an action plan*. The following chart provides examples of *powerful* and *platitudinous* new tunes.

Powerful	Platitudinous and "Pollyannaish"
"I can expect the best but if things go badly, I can handle it and try to relax."	"Everything will be okay."
"Being nervous just means I'm human. It doesn't mean I'll fail."	"I won't get nervous."
"Just because John was nasty doesn't mean I'm a geek. More kids think I'm nice than make fun of me. I can think of that when he bullies me."	"I don't care if John does not like me."

After the children write the new tune on the **Changing Your Tune Diary**, the therapist instructs the child to write down the new tune on an index card. We suggest the child write the event/stressor, feeling, and old tune on one side of the card and then write the new tune on the other side of the card. In this way, the child has a deck of coping statements to rely upon in specific situations.

The cards are very handy since they can fit in pockets, wallets, purses, notebooks, and so on. Moreover, index cards are very unobtrusive coping aids. Since children seem to enjoy writing on brightly colored cards, we recommend furnishing an assortment of colors. As children progress in the skill mastery, the different colors could be used to represent new tunes/coping thoughts in different situations or for different feelings (e.g., red = angry, blue = depressed or sad).

The **Changing Your Tune** activities teach the crucial skill of identifying events, feelings, thoughts (old tunes), and creating more adaptive thoughts (new tunes). The **Changing Your Tune Diary** is an ideal practice document the child can work on at home between the sessions. Completing several **Changing Your Tune Diaries** between meetings can serve to reinforce the new thinking patterns. With practice, the child will understand that his or her negative tunes can be changed.

Changing Your Tune

Tips for Children

PANDY SAYS

Have you ever listened to a song or a tune and couldn't get the words out of your mind? It's like you keep hearing them over and over inside your head.

Sometimes the things you say to yourself are like those words to the song. They keep playing over in your mind. They keep you stuck and stop you from doing things that make you feel better about yourself.

Many times the things you say to yourself when you are feeling mad, sad, worried, or scared make the feeling worse or last longer.

One time I was in school and no one wanted to play with me on the playground. I said to myself, "No one likes me. I'm a jerk." This was the same old tune I had been saying to myself.

I needed to say something else to help me with my feelings. So I thought and I thought. And I asked myself some questions. Finally, I said to myself, "Just because no one is playing with me today doesn't mean everyone doesn't like me. Sometimes kids play with me and sometimes they don't. If somebody doesn't play with me, it doesn't mean I'm a jerk. I can go play on the basketball court myself or go ask some kids if I can join them." *I changed my song and tune*.

See if you can change the things I wrote on my **Changing Your Tune Practice Diary** so I can *change my tune*. Then try some on your own.

Changing Your Tune Diary

(Practice Diary)

PANDY SAYS

1. Change the things I am saying to myself so my feelings will change.

2. Use your skills to come up with a new tune.

EVENT	FEELING	THOUGHT (Old Tune)	NEW THOUGHT (New Tune)
My parents yelled at me.	Sad	They don't love me.	Just because they yelled at me doesn't mean they don't love me. They are just mad right now.
Got a bad grade in school.	Sad	I'm stupid.	
I was picked last for a team at school.	Sad	Everybody thinks I'm awful.	
Say goodbye to my mom and dad at school.	Worried	I'm not going to be OK at school without my parents.	

EVENT	FEELING	THOUGHT (Old Tune)	NEW THOUGHT (Old Tune)
Getting ready for the day.	Scared	Something bad is going to happen.	
My parents are yelling at me.	Scared	I'll never be able to do it right. They won't love me anymore.	
My parents did not let me go over to my friend's house.	Mad	This is really unfair. They always tell me what to do.	

Changing Your Tune Diary

PANDY SAYS

1. Whenever you feel badly, write down the event, your feeling, and the old tunes that run through your mind.

2. Use your skills to come up with a new tune.

EVENT	FEELING	THOUGHT (Old Tune)	NEW THOUGHT (New Tune)

EVENT	FEELING	THOUGHT (Old Tune)	NEW THOUGHT (Old Tune)

Tease Whiz

GUIDELINES FOR THERAPISTS

Teasing is a common playground and school activity. However, anxious and depressed youngsters are often excruciatingly sensitive to children's barbs. They internalize rejection and fear negative evaluation. Often, they confuse others' opinions of themselves with fact. Indeed, confusing fact with opinion is an error common to highly approval-seeking individuals (Burns, 1980). Moreover, teasing may make depressed and anxious children feel small. They are likely to imagine the teaser as much larger and psychologically more powerful. Consequently, the **Tease Whiz** skill set helps children develop skills to separate fact from opinion and *shrink the teaser*.

The **Tease Whiz** skill set includes "Tips for Children," a sample **Tease Whiz Diary**, and a **Tease Whiz Diary**. Children are encouraged to read the "Tips for Children" and the therapist should process the guidelines with each child. Reviewing the **Tease Whiz Diary** sample should precede completing the **Tease Whiz Diary**.

Tease Whiz builds on several other skills. In order to complete the **Tease Whiz Diary**, children have to be able to identify their feelings and the accompanying thoughts. Additionally, children will need to be familiar with self-instructional and problem-solving strategies. In particular, **Tease Whiz** should follow **PANDY Coloring Sheets, My Mouse Traps and PANDY Fix-It, Catching Feelings and Thoughts**, and at least one other self-instructional technique (e.g., **Changing Your Tune**).

The **Tease Whiz** metaphor is a way to increase children's personal empowerment. Therapists should take time to set up the exercise by explaining what a WHIZ is. For example:

Therapist: Do you know what WHIZ means?
Child: No.
Therapist: A WHIZ is someone who can handle anything. A WHIZ is someone who is really an expert. You're going to learn to be an expert at handling teasing.

The object is to help the child identify with PANDY as a **Tease Whiz**. Therefore, therapists should be confident that the child understands the WHIZ concept. Certainly, reading the "Tips for Children" with each child will provide opportunities for understanding and identification.

The **Tease Whiz Sample Diary** begins with a description of the event ("Joey said I smelled bad"). The next step involves a PANDY SAYS question ("Who's in charge of my feelings?"). The child answers by circling either "I am" or "The other person is." This question helps the teased child regain a sense of control over their feelings. While they are unable to completely control the other child, they are nonetheless in control of their feelings. Accordingly, the personal empowerment coping skill is set in progress.

The third stage in **Tease Whiz** is based on a PANDY SAYS self-instruction. PANDY coaches the child to use his or her *just because* words. At this point, therapists should teach children the "*Just Because Skill*." Just because is based on a parsimonious but elegant technique described by Elliott (1991). The *Just Because* technique is "based on the assumption that much of clients' psychological suffering is related to the fusing together of two ideas between which there is no logical connection" (Elliott, 1991, p. 227). Teased children think that just because Billy called me a geek, it means that I am a geek. As Elliott rightly explains, the first part of the thought ("Billy called me a geek") is factual or accurate but the second part of the thought is evaluative ("It means I am a geek"). Therefore, the children can be taught to separate the two ideas they erroneously connected. Similarly to Elliott's description of his approach, children can be instructed to reinterpret the tease by inserting their "*just because*" words (e.g., "Just because Billy called me a geek, doesn't mean that I am one").

Step four involves another PANDY SAYS self-instruction. Children are encouraged to *shrink* the teaser. The shrink metaphor is another device designed to empower the teased child. This self-instruction helps children avoid defining themselves through the tease. The children are instructed to think about the other things that make up who they are. For instance, if a child is called a "doofus," they are asked to write what else other than a "doofus" defines who they are.

Stage 5 includes a different type of self-instruction. In this step, children are coached in *perspective-taking*. A typical and automatic reaction for teased children is to focus on themselves, their increasing self-consciousness, and their bad feelings. Thus, the perspective training is a way to distance the child from the tease. It moves the child from a painful subjective state to a more objective position. Therapists might want to provide children with information about "teasers." Children then could write down this information on a coping card. The following confabulated transcript illustrates the way therapists might provide this information to the children.

Therapist:	How do you suppose teasers feel about themselves?
Child:	I don't know.
Therapist:	Do you think they feel kind of good or not so good about themselves?
Child:	Not so good.
Therapist:	That's right. Teasers don't feel good about themselves so they want to make others feel bad about themselves. The worse you feel, the better the teaser feels. It's kind of like they feel small. So to build themselves up they have to cut others down. Does that make sense to you?

The **Tease Whiz Diary** concludes with a final PANDY SAYS self-instruction. In this last stage, children are prompted to develop a *problem-solving strategy*. Accordingly, **Tease Whiz** builds on the **Fix-It** skill set. Therapists should help the child generate action strategies to help them cope with the teasing. The following confabulated transcript illustrates the way therapists might help children develop a **Tease Whiz** thing to do.

Therapist:	It's probably pretty likely that Gretchen is going to continue to bug you and pick on you.
Child:	I know, I hate that.
Therapist:	Let's see if we can come up with a **Tease Whiz** thing to do.
Child:	I don't know how to do that.
Therapist:	Together maybe we can come up with a few things.
Child:	OK.
Therapist:	What did you learn from the **Tease Whiz Diary**?
Child:	Gretchen wants me to feel small.
Therapist:	That's a good start. Now what are you in charge of?
Child:	Whether I feel small or not.
Therapist:	Let's write that down. Gretchen wants to make you feel small but you are in charge of that.
Child:	That sounds good but what can I do?
Therapist:	What does **Tease Whiz** tell us?
Child:	Umm. Oh, I can shrink the teaser and walk away.
Therapist:	That's a good start. What else can you do?
Child:	I can use my "Just because" skills.
Therapist:	And say what?

Child:	Just because Gretchen thinks I'm stupid and clumsy doesn't mean I am.
Therapist:	What will help you walk away?
Child:	I guess knowing that just because Gretchen says something doesn't mean it's true.
Therapist:	If you walk away and say these things, I want you to give yourself a reward. Let's talk to mom and dad about what we could use.
Child:	That sounds great!

After the child has completed each step, the child can place their responses on cards. Placing their responses on cards makes the skills more portable. By transferring their responses to cards, the children can carry their responses with them. In this way, they may come in handy if the children are teased in school, on the bus, or on the playground.

The skills learned in **Tease Whiz** help the child define themselves as opposed to being defined by others. The youngster learns to think about the various traits that define himself/herself. Further, **Tease Whiz** educates children about the characteristics of those who tease others. By learning to "*shrink the teaser*" and use the "*just because*" words, the child has empowering techniques. Finally, *action plans* further increase children's self-control.

Tease Whiz

Tips for Children

PANDY SAYS

I know that some boys and girls like to tease other people. Many times when boys and girls tease me, I know they are just kidding me and I laugh along with them. Other times, if the teaser isn't kidding me, my feelings get hurt and I start to feel really badly. I wanted to learn how to handle the type of teasing that makes me feel badly.

I made up the **Tease Whiz Diary** to help me handle teasing. I called it **Tease Whiz** because a WHIZ is someone who is really good at handling things. I want to be a WHIZ at handling teasing. So, try the diary and you can learn to handle teasing, too.

Tease Whiz Diary

(Sample)

PANDY SAYS

What happened:

Joey said I smelled bad.

PANDY SAYS

Who's in charge of my feelings (circle one)?

  I am   The other person is

PANDY SAYS

Use your just because words:

Just because he said I smelled bad
doesn't mean I do. He is the only one
who ever says that.

List all the other things that make up who I am:

I am smart. I know PANDY skills!
I am friendly.
I can run fast.
I like to read.

Try to remember how teasers feel about themselves.

Teasers usually feel bad about themselves.
They really see themselves as very small
and tease others so they can feel big. I
CAN SHRINK THEM TO THEIR REAL
SIZE!

PANDY SAYS

Come up with a **Tease Whiz** thing to do:

Since I am in charge of my feelings, I am
going to ignore Joey's words. He doesn't
know me. He thinks he is big, but my
PANDY skills can shrink him.

Tease Whiz Diary

PANDY SAYS

What happened:

_____

_____

_____

PANDY SAYS

Who's in charge of my feelings (circle one)?

I am   The other person is

PANDY SAYS

Use your just because words:

_____

_____

_____

_____

PANDY SAYS

List all the other things that make up who I am:

_____

_____

_____

_____

Try to remember how teasers feel about themselves.

_____

_____

_____

_____

PANDY SAYS

Come up with a **Tease Whiz** thing to do:

_____

_____

_____

_____

Surf the Angry Sea

GUIDELINES FOR THERAPISTS

Surf the Angry Sea Diary is an activity focused on helping children manage their angry/irritable feelings. The exercise includes cognitive coping techniques based on the seminal work by Feindler and Ecton (1986), Goldstein et al. (1987), and Novaco (1979). Moreover, the activity makes use of a surfing metaphor to teach children coping skills. **Surfing the Angry Sea** is a technique which builds on the **Catching Feelings and Thoughts** and **Changing Your Tune** skill sets.

The surfing metaphor is based on the idea that strong feelings are similar to waves (Fidaleo & Southworth, 1992). The feelings build, crest, crash, and then gently roll to shore. However, children with anger management difficulties neglect this course of feelings and commonly engage in emotional reasoning (A. T. Beck, 1976; Burns, 1980). Emotional reasoning impels children to act on their anger. They experience anger as an aversive emotional state from which they want to escape. Children may impulsively act on their feelings as a way to relieve irritating internal pressures (A.T. Beck, 1976; Feindler & Ecton, 1986; Novaco, 1979).

The **Surf the Angry Sea Diary** emphasizes accepting and "riding out" the angry feelings without hurting oneself or others. The skill set includes a "Tips for Children," a sample completed diary, and a **Surf the Angry Sea Diary**. Therapists are encouraged to begin the sequence with the "Tips for Children," proceed to the sample diary, and then continue with the **Surf the Angry Sea Diary**.

The **Surf the Angry Sea Diary** begins with a self-monitoring module. First, children are taught to catch their angry feelings early before the wave builds in strength. Therapists may want to "play up" the surfing metaphor at this point. It may be helpful for therapists to discuss the way surfers catch a wave before it peaks. As children begin to realize the importance of *early identification of angry feelings*, therapists help children label the physiological, behavioral, and cognitive components of their anger. The therapist might ask questions such as the following:

- "What does your body feel like when you are angry?"
- "What do you do when you are angry?"
- "What goes through your mind when you are angry?"

Prompting children to be as specific as possible in their descriptions is an important aspect of this self-monitoring process. The sample diary provides a useful model for specificity. Therapists are well-advised to direct children's attention to the specific information included on the sample diary.

Step two on the **Surf the Angry Sea Diary** focuses on replacing anger producing cognitions with counter-thoughts that decrease angry arousal. The children are instructed to stop and create "cool" thoughts. Several examples of potential cool thoughts are provided on the diary. Therapists should invite children to read over the coping thoughts and circle ones that might work for them. At this point in the process, children might be asked to write any useful cool thoughts on index cards. As previously mentioned, transposing the coping statements onto cards provides additional opportunities for rehearsal and makes the coping statements more portable since children can carry the statements with them.

Step three on the diary involves children writing their own coping statements. Children are asked to create seven additional cool coping thoughts. After children write down their own coping thoughts, they are encouraged to write these thoughts on index cards as well.

Step four is the self-reward process. If the children manage their anger successfully, they deserve reinforcement! The self-reward is an opportunity for the child to create rewarding self-statements. Children are supplied with various examples of reinforcing self-statements. Of course, when children develop their own forms of self-reward, these self-statements tend to be more meaningful.

Finally, the child writes seven "self-congratulatory" phrases to praise himself or herself for handling their anger.

Surf the Angry Sea Diary is specifically designed to teach children how to effectively manage their angry thoughts and feelings. The diary uses the same principles that are taught in the other *Therapeutic Exercises for Children* exercises but tailors them specifically to angry feelings. The surfing metaphor is an action-oriented technique that engages youngsters. The four-step process ties together the identification of thoughts, feelings, and actions, and proceeds to creating adaptive thoughts to help the child manage his or her anger.

Surf the Angry Sea

Tips for Children

PANDY SAYS

Hello, boys and girls. Do you know how to surf? Have you ever seen anyone surf? Sometimes children who do not live by an ocean use a skateboard to surf! Have you ever done that? Sometimes, I like to pretend to surf even when I don't have a surfboard or a skateboard. Can you pretend to surf?

The reason I am talking about surfing is because I want to teach you how to **Surf the Angry Sea**. Anger is just like a wave in the ocean. Have you ever seen a wave? It rises slowly, building up power, and then comes into the shore with littler waves. To better deal with angry feelings, you have to ride them out. You have to learn to **Surf the Angry Sea**. When you **Surf the Angry Sea**, you stay ahead of the angry wave and don't get flooded by the feelings. How does that sound?

Here's what you do. First, you have to catch the wave early. This means pay attention to yourself when you first start getting angry. Watch out for your thoughts and actions. Next, relax and allow yourself to ride out the angry feelings. It might be a bumpy ride but hang on and keep your balance. Third, tell yourself things like, "*I need to stay in charge. Hitting someone makes me lose charge of myself.*"

Remember the angry feelings are like the waves. They may build up to big waves, but after a while they will become little waves. *If you can surf the angry sea without hurting yourself or someone else, you deserve a reward.* Make sure you give yourself one.

How does this plan sound to you? Be sure to ask your parents and counselors if you have any questions. Have a good ride!

Surf the Angry Sea Diary

(Sample)

PANDY SAYS

First, catch the wave. What does your body feel like when you are
angry? My body feels like:

I'm going to explode. Tense. My stomach
churns. I tighten up my fists.

What do you do when you are angry? When I am angry I:

Hit, scream, punch, and yell.

What goes through your mind when you are angry?

I'm going to get even. When I'm angry I have to
punch somebody. People shouldn't tell me what
to do   pops into my head.

Stop and think cool thoughts. Here are some cool thoughts that PANDY says:

- "Anger is like a wave."
- "I can surf the wave."
- "I need to stay in charge."
- "Hitting makes me lose charge of myself."
- "Staying in charge is the name of the game."
- "Anger builds up and crashes just like a wave. It doesn't last forever."

PANDY SAYS

Think of seven more cool thoughts:

1. Be cool and watch the wave.
2. Stay calm. The angry feelings will pass.
3. Be stronger than the angry feelings.
4. Keeping control defeats my anger.
5. Anger is just a feeling. I can stay in charge of it.
6. I can surprise my friends, myself, and my parents by staying calm.
7. I'm going to let the other person lose it by staying in charge, myself.

> NEXT, PUT ALL COOL THOUGHTS ON CARDS AND
> READ THEM OVER.

PANDY SAYS

Now, *praise yourself* if you surf the wave without hitting, yelling, or hurting yourself or somebody else. Here are some ways to praise yourself:

- "I was awesome."
- "I stayed in charge."
- "I was the boss of my angry feelings."
- "Hooray for me."
- "I used my mouse tools."

PANDY SAYS

Write down seven more things you can say to cheer yourself on!

1. Congratulations. I didn't scream at my brother.
2. Way to go! I surfed the wave.
3. I used my words to tell how angry I was! Terrific!
4. I knew I could ride out my anger.

5. <u>Fabulous! I didn't get flooded by the angry sea.</u>
6. <u>I kept control.</u>
7. <u>I kept cool. I put my anger on ice.</u>

PUT THESE CHEERS AND PRAISES ON CARDS.
BE SURE TO READ THEM OVER.

Surf the Angry Sea Diary

First, catch the wave. What does your body feel like when you are angry? My body feels like:

_____

_____

_____

What do you do when you are angry? When I am angry I:

_____

_____

_____

What goes through your mind when you are angry?

_____

_____

pops into my head.

_____

Stop and think cool thoughts. Here are some cool thoughts that PANDY says:

- "Anger is like a wave."
- "I can surf the wave."
- "I need to stay in charge."
- "Hitting makes me lose charge of myself."
- "Staying in charge is the name of the game."
- "Anger builds up and crashes just like a wave. It doesn't last forever."

PANDY SAYS

Think of seven more cool thoughts:

1. _____
2. _____
3. _____
4. _____
5. _____
6. _____
7. _____

> NEXT, PUT ALL COOL THOUGHTS ON CARDS AND
> READ THEM OVER.

PANDY SAYS

Now, *praise yourself* if you surf the wave without hitting, yelling, or hurting yourself or somebody else. Here are some ways to praise yourself:

- "I was awesome."
- "I stayed in charge."
- "I was the boss of my angry feelings."
- "Hooray for me."
- "I used my mouse tools."

PANDY SAYS

Write down seven more things you can say to cheer yourself on!

1. _____
2. _____
3. _____
4. _____

5. _____

6. _____

7. _____

| PUT THESE CHEERS AND PRAISES ON CARDS. |
| BE SURE TO READ THEM OVER. |

Techniques Requiring More In-Depth Rational Analysis

Clue Snooping

GUIDELINES FOR THERAPISTS

Tests of evidence are staples in cognitive-behavioral therapists' repertoires (A. T. Beck et al., 1979; J. S. Beck, 1995). A test of evidence is an elegant technique which involves depthful rational analysis. Procedures for conducting tests of evidence with adults have been described in detail by several authors (A. T. Beck et al., 1979; J. S. Beck, 1995; Padesky & Greenberger, 1995). Greenberger and Padesky (1995) presented a well-designed daily thought record which incorporates a test of evidence. Tests of evidence are especially useful when individuals' automatic thoughts reflect conclusions which are inaccurate generalizations and based on illogical foundations. The **Clue Snooping** skill set has "Tips for Children," a sample diary, and the **Clue Snooping Diary**.

Due to the cognitive and emotional processing demands, clinicians may mistakenly eschew tests of evidence. However, tests of evidence can be made simpler and more accessible to children. Thus, the **Clue Snooping Diary** was developed as a way to simplify tests of evidence and decrease cognitive/emotional processing demands. In short, tests of evidence can be fun!

Clue Snooping is a technique that should be used after children can identify feelings, thoughts, and events. Moreover, children should be well-practiced in the priming techniques and simpler self-instructional exercises such as **Changing Your Tune**, and **Me/Not Me**. Accordingly, **Clue Snooping** should be employed later in treatment.

The **Clue Snooping Diary** makes use of a magnifying glass icon and relies on a detective metaphor. Detective metaphors are commonly used in cognitive-behavioral work with children (Kendall, 1988). The child first captures the thought/belief they want to test. The thought or belief is written in the thought bubble. In the second step of the process, children list the clues that make them think the thought is true. Thirdly, children list the clues that convince them the thought or belief is not true. Next, the children compare the clues and come up with a conclusion based on the two sets of clues. After the children construct a conclusion, they add a problem-solving and action component. Finally, the children rerate their feeling.

When the **Clue Snooping Diary** is introduced, therapists are well-advised to integrate the detective metaphor in their clinical work with this exercise. Bringing a magnifying glass or a detective hat to the session is a good strategy. Examining everyday items for clues or fingerprints is a fun way to play detective. After the "detective play" is finished, the therapist can introduce the diary. Key introductory and processing questions could include:

- "What do detectives do?"
- "What is a detective's job?"
- "Detectives 'snoop' for clues. Do you know what 'snoop' means? It kind of means being nosy or curious to find out about things."
- "How would you like to snoop for clues?"

At this time, the "Tips for Children" could be presented. Reviewing the tips with the youngsters and making sure they understand the task is a good idea. Connecting the metaphor to the task will increase the technique's impact. Moreover, helping children see the value of **Clue Snooping** in their own lives will increase their investment in the task.

Introducing the task via the sample diary is a natural next step. The therapist directs the child's attention to the negative thought listed in the thought bubble (e.g., "I'm stupid"). At this point, the therapist may elect to ask children if they ever had this thought go through their mind. Therapists and children then connect the thoughts to their accompanying feelings. In the next stage, therapists and children review the clues that support the negative belief. Subsequently, they review the clues that do not support the belief.

Coming to a conclusion is the crucial next step. The child is required to interpret or analyze both the clues that support the thought and the clues that do not support the belief. It is important for the child to depthfully process both sections. Comparing the two sets of clues will give the child added perspective. The child should weigh both sections when making a conclusion. Balancing the evidence recorded both for and opposed to the thought facilitates depthful processing. Therapists should work diligently to ensure the child makes sense of the negative evidence. If the child's conclusions do not account for the negative evidence, the believability of new conclusions may be compromised.

Once the child has constructed a conclusion, a *problem-solving* or *action plan* is developed. In the action plan, a problem-solving strategy is developed in response to the clues supporting the negative belief. For instance, in the sample diary, the child needed to study and check over homework. Adding a problem-solving strategy improves the believability of the **Clue Snooping** conclusion and empowers the child. Finally, children rerate their new feeling which accompanies the conclusion and problem-solving strategy.

We offer several additional recommendations for the **Clue Snooping Diary**. First, most children will need help listing the clues that convince them their thought is true. Therapists might ask some questions such as:

- "What things convince you that your thought is true?"
- "What things persuade you that your thought is true?"
- "What things make you think that your thought is true?"
- "What things show you that your thought is true?"

Secondly, trying to preempt the clues that support the negative thought is a natural urge for therapists. However, therapists are well-advised to resist this urge. Rather, children should be encouraged to fully articulate all the clues that buttress their belief. Accordingly, after the list is seemingly exhausted, the therapist should once again check-in with the child and ask, *"Is there anything else you would like to add before we move on?"*

Clue Snooping is an important cognitive skill that helps children determine whether their thoughts and beliefs are accurate or inaccurate. The detective metaphor adds an element of fun and challenge to this task. By completing each step in the **Clue Snooping Diary**, the youngster systematically learns to evaluate the accuracy of their explanations and conclusions. After determining if their thoughts are accurate or inaccurate the child can create a plan for change. By combining *thought testing*, *creating an action plan*, and finally *rerating of feelings* the child creates a clear blueprint for change.

Clue Snooping

Tips for Children

PANDY SAYS

Hi! It's me, **PANDY**, the Mouse-in-the-House. Have any of you played detective or scientist? Well, I have and let me tell you it sure is fun. Scientists and detectives *"Snoop for Clues."* That's right, they are *Nosy! Nooosy! Really Really Nosy!*

That's what I want you to learn. I want you all to be *Really Nosy* about what pops into your mind and how you explain things. So, we are all going to be *Nosy, Nosy Detectives* and find out whether the way we explain what happens to us is the most correct. How does that sound?

We have to *snoop for clues* in a special way. We have to look for **FACTS**. Remember: We are looking for *Just the Facts*! Talk to your counselor about what a **Fact** is.

Now, let's go snooping.

My friend Keisha thought that no one liked her. She felt really SAD! She asked me to help her find out if it was *true* that no one liked her. We needed to look for *clues*.

Now, where would you look for clues? What questions could you ask to find clues? The questions I asked Keisha were:

- "Who do you know who does not like you? List all the kids you know who do not like you."
- "How do you know that they don't like you?"
- "Who do you know that really likes you? List all the kids you know who like you."
- "How do you know that they like you?"
- "If you have some people who like you, then how is it correct that 'No one likes you?'"

To find clues, you have to ask questions like these:

- "What makes me believe this thought <u>is</u> totally, completely, absolutely correct?"
- "Is there another explanation for these clues?"
- "What makes me believe this thought <u>is not</u> completely, absolutely, totally correct?"

Take a look at another example I wrote out on my diary. Talk with your parents and counselors if you have more questions about being a **Clue Snooper.**

Clue Snooping Diary

(Sample)

I want to find clues about this thought:

Clues I found that make me think this thought <u>is</u> totally true.

I got 3 C's on my report card.
The other kids laughed when I got the answers wrong
in math class.
My mom and dad said they were disappointed in me.
My brother got all A's.

Clues I found that make me think this thought <u>is not</u> totally true.

I got 3 B's and 1 A in my other classes.
My teachers and parents tell me I'm a hard worker.
One of my stories was in the school paper.
I only got one C on my last report card.

Now that I have SNOOPED FOR CLUES, what do I believe NOW?

I am not really stupid.
I did not do as well as I usually do On
my report card.
I felt bad because my mom and dad were
disappointed but I know they still love me.

What can I do differently NOW?

I didn't study as much as I have in the past.
I need to make sure I study before I watch TV.
I need to check over my work and ask the
teacher if I am not sure about how to
do my homework.

How do I feel NOW?

A little guilty and sad, but not as
bad as I did before.

Clue Snooping Diary

I want to find clues about this thought:

Clues I found that make me think this thought <u>is</u> totally true.

_____

_____

_____

_____

_____

Clues I found that make me think this thought <u>is not</u> totally true.

_____

_____

_____

_____

_____

Now that I have SNOOPED FOR CLUES, what do I believe NOW?

_____

_____

_____

_____

_____

What can I do differently NOW?

_____

_____

_____

_____

_____

How do I feel NOW?

_____

_____

_____

_____

_____

EXERCISE 16

Real or False Alarms

GUIDELINES FOR THERAPISTS

The **Real or False Alarms Diary** is an exercise designed to test children's catastrophic predictions. Anxious children worry that bad things will happen to them and expect that they will not be able to cope with the negative event once it occurs (A. T. Beck & Clark, 1988; Kendall et al., 1992; Vasey, 1993). The metaphor of "false alarms" is offered to describe children's anxious behavior (A. T. Beck, 1976). Children expect that their worries represent real alarms and engage in various avoidance behaviors. While some worries may in fact represent real alarms, most worries are false alarms for anxious children. The **Real or False Alarms Diary** helps children discern real from false alarms as well as develop a problem-solving strategy should a real alarm occur.

The **Real or False Alarms** skill set includes "Tips for Children," a sample **Real or False Alarms Diary,** and a **Real or False Alarms Diary**. Therapists should begin with a discussion of real and false alarms, present the sample diary, begin the **Real or False Alarms Diary** in session, and give the child the assignment to complete the diary for mousework. **Real or False Alarms** should follow self-monitoring tasks such as **Diamond Connections**, **Bubble Up Your Fear** or **Catching Feelings and Thoughts**, as well as a self-instructional skill such as **Changing Your Tune**.

Children can readily understand the real and false alarm metaphors. Accordingly, therapists are encouraged to embellish the real and false alarm metaphor. Toy fire engines with electronic sirens could be brought into the session. Therapists and children could mimic the whining sound of a siren. In our PANDY school-based groups, we brought in plastic fire chief hats for the children to wear when they complete the diaries. By connecting the diary to the playful experiences, each of these augmentations may help the children remember the concepts. Therapists are also encouraged to engage children in animated discussions of real and false alarms. Therapists might ask questions such as:

- "What is a real alarm?"
- "What is a false alarm?"
- "What is the difference between a real alarm and a false alarm?"
- "What happens if the fire department thinks it is a real alarm when it is a false alarm?"
- "What happens if the fire department thinks it is a false alarm when it is a real alarm?"
- "What is important about telling the difference between real and false alarms?"

Therapists should now try to help children connect the real and false alarms to their worries. The "Tips for Children" can help youngsters link real and false alarms with worries. Therapists might ask discussion questions such as:

- "How are your worries like real alarms?"
- "How are your worries like false alarms?"
- "Which of your worries are real alarms?"
- "Which of your worries are false alarms?"
- "How can you tell the difference?"
- "What is important about knowing whether your worry is a real or false alarm?"

Introducing the "Tips for Children" and sample **Real or False Alarms Diary** is a natural next step. Children may then read the "Tips for Children" text aloud and the PANDY SAYS text on the diary. Similarly to other "Tips" sections, therapists should devote time to ensure that the child understands the material. The therapist should review each point in the PANDY SAYS section with the child (e.g., list your worries for the week) and highlight the relevant example. Children should be encouraged to be as specific as possible when listing their worries. When the children come to the part where they mark whether the worries are real alarms or false alarms, therapists should be sure to check that the children realize they have to *wait until the feared event passes to know whether the worry was a real or false alarm.*

After the child understands how to mark whether their worries were real or false alarms, therapists may move on to the next section on the diary. Children simply need to count the number of real alarms and false alarms and then compare the two totals. Based on this comparison, two questions are asked:

- "What did you do to handle the REAL ALARMS?"
- "If you had more FALSE ALARMS, what does that mean about whether the things you worry about will come true?"

The first question helps children develop a coping response when they experience a real alarm. The second question helps children develop a new way to evaluate their worries. Responses to each of these questions could be written on index cards.

The **Real or False Alarms Diary** clearly illustrates whether the child is worrying needlessly about events that rarely occur. The diary provides children with a clearer view of the accuracy of their fears. By monitoring worries on the diary as well as tracking their occurrence, youngsters earn greater self-control. The final sections of the **Real or False Alarms Diary** hone the children's problem-solving skills and abilities to counter catastrophic thinking.

Real or False Alarms

Tips for Children

PANDY SAYS

Hi, kids. It's me, **PANDY**. The **Real or False Alarms Diary** helps you decide if your problems and worries are real or not. Sometimes I worry about things that never actually happen. Do you ever do that? This diary helped me learn that I was spending way too much time worrying about things that I don't need to worry about, because they never happened.

The first thing you do is list your worries for the week. Then, wait a week to see if your worries were **REAL ALARMS** (they really happened) or **FALSE ALARMS** (they didn't happen). The next part is easy. Just count up the number of real and false alarms. Answer the question, "*Did you have more REAL ALARMS or FALSE ALARMS?*" Look at my example to help you with this diary.

Then, write how you handled your real worries. What did you do, think, or say to manage your worries? Finally, if you did have more false alarms than real alarms, what does that tell you about what you're worrying about? This diary shows you that you may be worrying needlessly about some things and that you may know how to handle your other worries. When you learn how to handle your feelings you will feel better about yourself and what you do. Good luck conquering your worries!

Real or False Alarms Diary

(Sample)

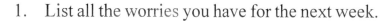

PANDY SAYS

1. List all the worries you have for the next week.

2. **At the end of the week**, decide whether the worry was a **REAL ALARM** (the thing you worried about happened) or a **FALSE ALARM** (the thing you worried about did not happen).

3. After you decide, put a check under the column you choose.

4. Use my questions to help you come to a conclusion.

Worries for the Week	Real Alarm (It really happened)	False Alarm (Didn't really happen)
Jenny will be mean to me.		✓
I will do badly in spelling.		✓
No one will play with me at recess.	✓	
I will get nervous when I read my book report.	✓	
I will say something dumb at lunch.		✓
I will call Jose to come over and he'll say no.		✓

How many of your worries were **REAL ALARMS**? _2_

How many of your worries were **FALSE ALARMS**? _4_

Did you have more **REAL ALARMS** or **FALSE ALARMS**?

more false alarms

What did you do to handle the **REAL ALARMS**?

I didn't have more real alarms. I handled being nervous by breathing slowly. and just thinking about what I was reading. I remembered that being nervous is normal. I played by myself at recess and the next day I made plans with someone to play together.

If you had more **FALSE ALARMS**, what does that mean about whether the things you worry about will come true?

Most of my worries did not come true. Maybe most of the things I worry about don't come true.

PANDY

Real or False Alarms Diary

1. List all the worries you have for the next week.

2. **At the end of the week**, decide whether the worry was a **REAL ALARM** (the thing you worried about happened) or a **FALSE ALARM** (the thing you worried about did not happen).

3. After you decide, put a check under the column you choose.

4. Use my questions to help you come to a conclusion.

Worries for the Week	Real Alarm (It really happened)	False Alarm (Didn't really happen)

How many of your worries were **REAL ALARMS**?_____

How many of your worries were **FALSE ALARMS**? _____

Did you have more **REAL ALARMS** or **FALSE ALARMS**?

_____

What did you do to handle the **REAL ALARMS**?

_____

_____

_____

_____

_____

If you had more **FALSE ALARMS**, what does that mean about whether the things you worry about will come true?

_____

_____

_____

_____

Breaking the Crystal Ball

GUIDELINES FOR THERAPISTS

The **Breaking the Crystal Ball Diary** emphasizes testing out and countering catastrophic predictions. The skill set includes "Tips for Children," **Breaking the Crystal Ball Sample Diary,** and a **Breaking the Crystal Ball Diary** in which children evaluate their catastrophic predictions. Therapists begin the process by explaining *Crystal Ball Thinking*, reviewing the "Tips for Children" and **Sample Diary**, and helping the child apply the blank diary to their own catastrophic predictions.

Anxious and depressed children tend to make negative predictions about the future. Cognitive therapists commonly term these inaccuracies *catastrophizing, fortunetelling*, and *mind reading* (A. T. Beck et al., 1979; J. S. Beck, 1995; Burns, 1980). In essence, children make predictions about the future and act on these predictions as if they have some special ability to see the future. These predictions become reified and assume the power to shape children's thoughts, feelings, and behavior despite their unreliability.

We elected to teach children about this process through a crystal ball metaphor. First, the crystal ball metaphor is easily understood by most children. They are familiar with magicians, gypsies, 8-balls, and fortunetelling. Secondly, the crystal ball metaphor nicely communicates the concept of "magical thinking" which permeates many anxious children's cognitive processes. Thirdly, the notion of using a crystal ball provides distance and psychological safety for the child. The inaccurate prognostications are not personal mistakes but rather a function of relying on unreliable means to make predictions. In sum, the metaphor supplies valuable advantages.

The **Breaking the Crystal Ball** skill set is a relatively elegant and complex exercise. We recommend that therapists use this technique with children after the youngsters have learned to identify situations, thoughts, and feelings. Moreover, children should be experienced with the **Changing Your Tune** skill set. Thus, **Breaking the Crystal Ball** is an exercise best timed for the later treatment stages.

The **Breaking the Crystal Ball Diary** includes a series of questions that lead children through the process of examining their negative predictions. First, children identify their negative prediction ("What do I fear will happen?"). Next, they connect their belief to their feelings ("How will I feel if it happens?"). Thirdly, they record what really happened. Following their description of what happened, they note the coping strategies they employed. Finally, they rerate their feeling after they faced the predicted stressor.

The second part of the diary directly challenges their crystal ball thinking. The crystal ball thinking is initially tested through successive yes or no questions.

- "Did what I expect to happen really happen?"
- "Did this surprise me?"
- "Was my crystal ball wrong?"
- "If my crystal ball was wrong, do I think I should still use it?"

The child is then asked to supply a reason for eliminating the crystal ball or keeping it. The next steps in the process deal with the possibility that some negative predictions are accurate. If the child's negative prediction came true, the child records the ways he or she coped with the unfortunate outcome. Further, the child is subsequently asked to make a conclusion regarding their own capacity to cope with desirable outcomes. Finally, based on the preceding work and analysis, children are asked to circle an option indicating whether they are in charge of the fear or their fear is in charge of them.

Like many of the other exercises and worksheets in this workbook, **Breaking the Crystal Ball Sample Diary** illustrates how to complete the diary. The sample provides a model for children to follow. As therapists review the example diary with the children, they should make liberal use of the crystal ball metaphor. Therapists may elect to make a crystal ball to reify the metaphor. Additionally, therapists and children could role-play being fortunetellers.

This exercise helps to minimize excessive worry and reduce the accompanying anticipatory anxiety. The technique also builds children's ability to handle difficult situations. The crystal ball metaphor prompts children to objectively evaluate their catastrophic predictions. Analyzing youngsters' predictions in a playful manner reduces their defensiveness and helps them gain needed distance from their worries. With continued practice, children can learn to assess the reliability of their catastrophic predictions and subsequently come to doubt their dire prognostications.

Breaking The Crystal Ball

Tips for Children

PANDY SAYS

Do you know what a fortuneteller is? Have you ever seen a movie about a fortuneteller? Have you ever read a book about a fortuneteller? Have you ever been to a circus or fair and seen a fortuneteller?

Fortunetellers think they can see into the future. They think they can guess what is going to happen. Do you ever think you know what is going to happen? What things do you guess will happen in the future?

Many times when children get worried, they predict or guess that something bad might happen in the future. That is their worry talking. When boys and girls become overly worried, they think the worst might happen even before it ever does. Does this ever happen to you?

Fortunetellers often use a crystal ball. They magically believe the crystal ball will correctly tell the future. When you worry something bad might happen, you are really relying on your crystal ball. You expect that the crystal ball is correct. But you have to be a more watchful fortuneteller. You have to figure out when your crystal ball is correct or not. If your crystal ball is guessing correctly and works well for you, you don't have to do anything differently. But when it is not working well and your worries about the future do not help you, you need to *break that crystal ball*.

Here's how to break the crystal ball. First, write down the bad thing that you guess will happen that makes you worried. Next, write down the feeling that goes along with your guess. After this, write down what really happened. Have fun *"breaking the crystal ball."*

Breaking The Crystal Ball Diary

(Sample)

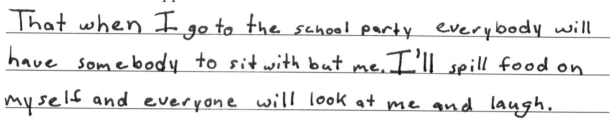

PANDY SAYS

My crystal ball thinking tells me what I fear will happen.
What do I fear will happen?

That when I go to the school party everybody will have somebody to sit with but me. I'll spill food on myself and everyone will look at me and laugh.

How will I feel if it happens?

Scared, embarrassed, and sad

What really happened?

I sat with some other kids. We all laughed at jokes. I forgot to worry about spilling.

What did I do to make things work out?

I smiled at some kids and asked if I could sit with them. I paid attention to the kids' jokes and tried to ignore my worries about spilling.

How did I feel?

Not so scared or embarrassed. OK.

Did what I expect to happen really happen (circle one)?

       YES   (NO)

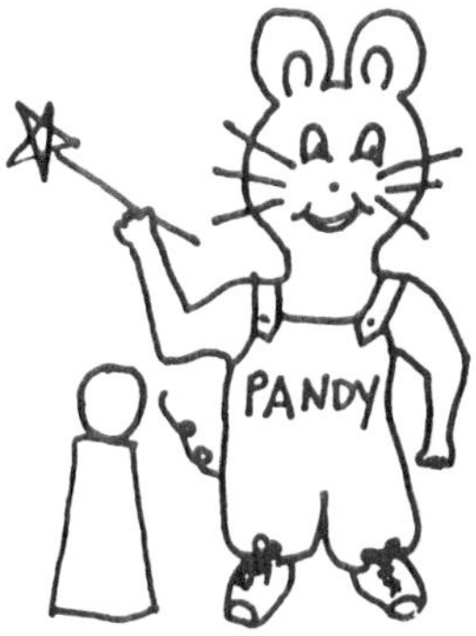

Did this surprise me (circle one)?

       (YES)   NO

Was my crystal ball right (circle one)?

       YES   (NO)

If my crystal ball was wrong, do I think I should still use it (circle one)?

       YES   (NO)

What's my reason?

My crystal ball was wrong. It does not tell the future well. It does not work for me.

If my crystal ball was right, what did I do to make things work out for myself?

My crystal ball was wrong.

If I made things work out for myself, what does that say about me?

I can do things to make friends. Just becquse I think I am going to embarrass myself doesn't mean I will.

If the thing I feared happened but I made it work out for myself, am I in charge of my fear or is my fear in charge of me (circle one)?

(I am in charge of my fear.)

My fear is in charge of me.

Breaking The Crystal Ball Diary

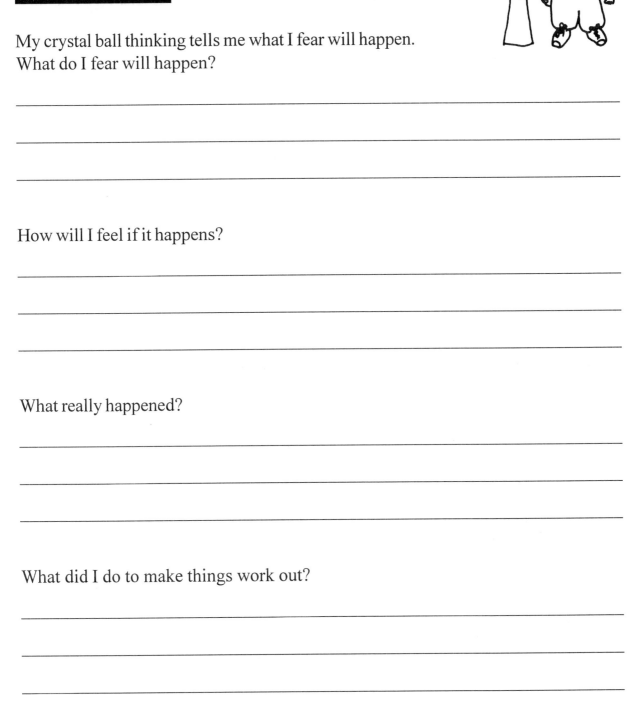

PANDY SAYS

My crystal ball thinking tells me what I fear will happen.
What do I fear will happen?

_____

_____

_____

How will I feel if it happens?

_____

_____

_____

What really happened?

_____

_____

_____

What did I do to make things work out?

_____

_____

_____

How did I feel?

_____

_____

_____

Did what I expect to happen really happen (circle one)?

      YES   NO

Did this surprise me (circle one)?

      YES   NO

Was my crystal ball right (circle one)?

      YES   NO

If my crystal ball was wrong, do I think I should still use it (circle one)?

      YES   NO

What's my reason?

_____

_____

_____

If my crystal ball was right, what did I do to make things work out for myself?

_____

_____

_____

If I made things work out for myself, what does that say about me?

_____

_____

_____

If the thing I feared happened but I made it work out for myself, am I in charge of my fear or is my fear in charge of me (circle one)?

I am in charge of my fear.

My fear is in charge of me.

Thought Digger

GUIDELINES FOR THERAPISTS

The most elegant goal of the *Therapeutic Exercises for Children* workbook is constructing questions to challenge distressing automatic thoughts. **Thought Digger** is a fun way to teach children this self-questioning process. **Thought Digger** modifies both cognitive content and cognitive process. The **Thought Digger** questions derail the negative automatic thought process prompting children to objectively evaluate their beliefs rather than dutifully accepting them as facts. The questions help structure the child's counter-thoughts. By answering the questions, children are able to construct an adaptive response.

Accessing questions which challenge automatic thoughts is a difficult task. Our clinical experience suggests that youngsters need help acquiring these questions. **Thought Digger** is roughly based on the Challenging Questions Worksheets developed by Calhoun and Resick (1993) and supplies children with questions they can ask themselves. Once they acquire the questions, the **Thought Digger Diary** also encourages children to apply these questions to their self-critical thoughts.

Thought Digging is an active coping skill. **The Thought Digger** skills are presented in two phases. In phase one, **Thought Digger Questions**, 11 sample questions are listed for children's perusal. The children read over the questions and then add additional questions. In phase two, **Thought Digger Diary**, children record the stressful event, feeling, and thought in the first three columns. In the fourth column, the child selects a question to ask himself/herself by circling a prepared question contained in the last column.

The thought digging process can be fun for children. Thought digging is similar to the scientific process and therapists are invited to augment this metaphor. We encourage children to see themselves as *archeologists who dig for clues*. Children may also resonate to the idea of being a *thought detective*.

We have found it useful for children to mimic digging action when they first learn the skills. For example, therapists invite the children to become Thought Diggers and pick up an imaginary shovel. Connecting an abstract concept with a concrete action helps children's recall. Therapists can subsequently prompt the questioning by simply mimicking the digging action. Moreover, thought digging can become a therapeutic shorthand. Instead of asking children questions such as "Did you evaluate your thought?," therapists might ask, "*Are you being a Thought Digger*?"

Thought Digger teaches self-questioning skills. The self-questioning process increases the child's ability to accurately assess his or her thoughts and the accompanying feelings. The graduated nature of this activity simplifies the scientific questioning process into two parts with the two-page skill set. After answering the **Thought Digger Questions**, the second part expands to include a modified thought diary or **Thought Digger Diary**. The **Thought Digger** metaphor adds fun to the therapeutic equation. Thus, the sequential nature of this activity prepares children to better analyze the accuracy of their distressing thoughts and feelings.

Thought Digger

Tips for Children

PANDY SAYS

Hi, boys and girls! Have you ever dug a hole in the sand or dirt? Did you ever find anything in that hole? It's kind of fun to dig for treasure or dig for clues. Digging for clues is what my next diary is about. I'm going to teach you to be a **Thought Digger**. When you are a **Thought Digger**, you will learn to hunt for clues so you can *check out your thoughts and see if they are true.*

The first three steps are things you already know how to do. First, you write down the event. Second, write down your feelings and then write down what is going through your mind. Now, you are ready to hunt for clues and be a **Thought Digger**.

On the last column of my diary, I have listed lots of **Thought Digger Questions**. Take a look at these questions and pick a few that you think will be helpful to ask yourself. Circle the questions you have picked. Once you have asked yourself these questions, try to hunt for an answer to them. When you have hunted for clues, you have a new way to think about the event. If the question is helpful, you may want to write it down on a card so you can remember to ask yourself these **Thought Digger Questions**. Now you are a **Thought Digger**. Go ahead and try it out. Happy hunting!!

Thought Digger Questions

When you notice yourself feeling badly, and catch your thoughts that go along with these feelings, be sure to ask yourself some questions. Here are some questions for your toolbox:

1. What good things about myself am I ignoring?

2. What good things about other people am I ignoring?

3. Are there other ways to think about the event?

4. How do I know for sure that my thoughts are true?

5. Am I using my feelings as facts?

6. Am I expecting too much from myself?

7. Am I expecting too little from myself?

8. Am I thinking that a bad thing is sure to happen when I really don't know?

9. Am I confusing "maybe" with "for sure?"

10. Am I blaming myself?

11. Am I blaming others?

Think of some other **Thought Digger Questions** to ask yourself:

_____

_____

_____

_____

_____

Thought Digger Diary

(Sample)

EVENT	FEELING	THOUGHT	THOUGHT DIGGER QUESTIONS
My friends did better on their tests than I did.	Embarrassed	Everybody else is smarter than I am.	Circle the questions to ask yourself. • (Are there other ways to think about the event?) • (What good things about myself am I ignoring?) • (Am I using my feelings as facts?) • Am I looking at all the facts? • Am I expecting too much from myself? • Am I expecting too little from myself? • Am I blaming others? • Am I expecting too much from others? • Am I expecting the worst to happen? • Am I thinking something is permanent when it is really temporary? • Am I blaming myself or am I taking responsibility? • How do I know for sure this will happen?

Thought Digger Diary

EVENT	FEELING	THOUGHT	THOUGHT DIGGER QUESTIONS
			Circle the questions to ask yourself. • Are there other ways to think about the event? • What good things about myself am I ignoring? • Am I using my feelings as facts? • Am I looking at all the facts? • Am I expecting too much from myself? • Am I expecting too little from myself? • Am I blaming others? • Am I expecting too much from others? • Am I expecting the worst to happen? • Am I thinking something is permanent when it is really temporary? • Am I blaming myself or am I taking responsibility? • How do I know for sure this will happen?

References

Beck, A. T. (1976). *Cognitive Therapy and the Emotional Disorders.* New York: International Universities Press.

Beck, A. T. (1985). Cognitive therapy, behavior therapy, psychoanalysis, and pharmacotherapy: A cognitive continuum. In M. J. Mahoney & A. Freeman (Eds.), *Cognition and Psychotherapy* (pp. 325-347). New York: Plenum.

Beck, A. T., & Clark, D. A. (1988). Anxiety and depression: An information processing perspective. *Anxiety Research: An International Journal, 1,* 23-36.

Beck, A. T., Rush, A. J., Shaw, B. F., & Emery, G. (1979). *Cognitive Therapy of Depression: A Treatment Manual.* New York: Guilford.

Beck, J. S. (1995). *Cognitive Therapy: Basics and Beyond.* New York: Guilford.

Burns, D. D. (1980). *Feeling Good: The New Mood Therapy.* New York: Signet.

Calhoun, K. S., & Resick, P. A. (1993). Post-traumatic stress disorder. In D. H. Barlow (Ed.), *Clinical Handbook of Psychological Disorders* (pp. 48-98). New York: Guilford.

Daley, M. F. (1969). The "Reinforcement Menu": Finding effective reinforcers. In J. D. Krumboltz & C. E. Thoreson (Eds.), *Behavioral Counseling: Cases and Techniques* (pp. 42-45). New York: Holt, Rinehart, & Winston.

D'Zurilla, T. J. (1986). *Problem-Solving Therapy: A Social Competence Approach to Clinical Intervention.* New York: Springer Publishing.

Elliott, J. (1991). Defusing conceptual fusions: The "just because" technique. *Journal of Cognitive Psychotherapy, 5,* 227-229.

Feindler, E. L., & Ecton, R. B. (1986). *Adolescent Anger Control: Cognitive-Behavioral Techniques.* New York: Pergamon.

Fidaleo, R. A., & Southworth, S. (1992, June). *Understanding and Treating Agoraphobia From a Cognitive Perspective.* Grand rounds presentation delivered at Mesa Vista Hospital, San Diego, CA.

Friedberg, R. D. (1993). Inpatient cognitive therapy: Games cognitive therapists play. *The Behavior Therapist, 16,* 41-42.

Friedberg, R. D., Crosby, L. E., Friedberg, B. A., Rutter, J. G., & Knight, K. R. (1999). Making cognitive-behavior therapy user-friendly for children. *Cognitive and Behavioral Practice, 6,* 189-200.

Friedberg, R. D., Mason, C., & Fidaleo, R. A. (1992). *Switching Channels: A Cognitive-Behavioral Workjournal for Adolescents.* Odessa, FL: Psychological Assessment Resources.

Goldstein, A. P., Glick, B., Reiner, S., Zimmerman, D., & Coultry, T. M. (1987). *Aggression Replacement Training: A Comprehensive Intervention for Aggressive Youth.* Champaign, IL: Research Press.

Greenberger, D., & Padesky, C. A. (1995). *Mind Over Mood.* New York: Guilford.

Jaycox, L. H., Reivich, K. J., Gillham, J. E., & Seligman, M. E. P. (1994). Prevention of depressive symptoms in school children. *Behavior Research and Therapy, 32,* 801-816.

Kendall, P. C. (1988). *The Stop and Think Workbook.* Philadelphia, PA: Temple University.

Kendall, P. C., Chansky, T. E., Kane, M. T., Kim, R. S., Kortlander, E., Ronan, K. R., Sessa, F. M., & Siqueland, L. (1992). *Anxiety Disorders in Youth: Cognitive-Behavioral Interventions.* Boston: Allyn & Bacon.

Masters, J. C., Burish, T. G., Hollon, S. D., & Rimm, D. C. (1987). *Behavior Therapy: Techniques and Empirical Findings* (2nd ed.). San Diego, CA: Harcourt, Brace, Jovanovich.

Meichenbaum, D. H. (1985). *Stress Inoculation Training.* New York: Pergamon.

Nolen-Hoeksema, S., & Girgus, J. S. (1995). Explanatory style, achievement, depression, and gender differences in childhood and early adolescence. In G. M. Buchanan & M. E. P. Seligman (Eds.), *Explanatory Style* (pp. 57-70). New York: Lawrence Erlbaum.

Nolen-Hoeksema, S., Girgus, J. S., & Seligman, M. E. P. (1996). Predictors and consequences of childhood depressive symptoms: A 5 year longitudinal study. *Journal of Abnormal Psychology, 101,* 405-422.

Novaco, R. W. (1979). The cognitive regulation of anger and stress. In P. C. Kendall & S. D. Hollon (Eds.), *Cognitive-Behavioral Interventions: Theory, Research, and Procedures* (pp. 241-285). New York: Academic Press.

Padesky, C. A., & Greenberger, D. (1995). *A Clinician's Guide to Mind Over Mood.* New York: Guilford.

Phillips, D., Fischer, S. C., & Singh, R. (1977). A children's reinforcement survey schedule. *Journal of Behavior Therapy and Experimental Psychiatry, 8,* 131-134.

Riskind, J. H. (1991). A set of cognitive priming interventions for cognitive therapy homework exercises. *The Behavior Therapist, 14,* 43.

Riskind, J. H., Sarampote, C. S., & Mercier, M. A. (1996). For every malady a sovereign cure: Optimism training. *Journal of Cognitive Psychotherapy, 10,* 105-118.

Seligman, M. E. P., Reivich, K., Jaycox, L., & Gillham, J. E. (1995). *The Optimistic Child.* Boston: Houghton & Mifflin.

Silverman, W. K., & Kurtines, W. M. (1996). *Anxiety and Phobic Disorders: A Pragmatic Approach.* New York: Plenum.

Spiegler, M. D., & Guevremont, D. C. (1998). *Contemporary Behavior Therapy* (3rd ed.). Pacific Grove, CA: Brooks/Cole.

Spivack, G., Platt, J. J., & Shure, M. B. (1976). *The Problem-Solving Approach to Adjustment.* San Francisco: Jossey-Bass.

Stark, K. D. (1990). *Childhood Depression: School-Based Intervention.* New York: Guilford.

Vasey, M. W. (1993). Development and cognition in childhood anxiety. In T. H. Ollendick & R. J. Prinz (Eds.), *Advances in Clinical Child Psychology* (Vol. 15, pp. 1-39). New York: Plenum.

Wellman, H. M., Hollander, M., & Schult, C. A. (1996). Young children's understanding of thought bubbles and of thought. *Child Development, 67,* 768-788.

Please visit us online at:

http://www.prpress.com

This website contains:

- ✓ Descriptions of all of our titles with
  - • complete tables of contents
  - • reviews of our books
  - • author biographies
- ✓ Online ordering
- ✓ Online queries and requests for catalogs
- ✓ Information on our home-study continuing education programs
- ✓ Our publishing guidelines
- ✓ The history of our company

. . . . and much, much more!

- -

Catalog Request

For our latest catalog and ordering information, please write, call, fax, or e-mail the following information:

Name: _____
PLEASE PRINT CLEARLY

Address (Company name if business address): _____

Address: _____

City/State/Zip: _____ Country: _____

Phone Number: _____ E-mail: _____

I am a (check one):
- ❑ Psychologist
- ❑ Clinical Social Worker
- ❑ Marriage and Family Therapist
- ❑ Mental Health Counselor

- ❑ School Psychologist
- ❑ Psychiatrist
- ❑ Parent
- ❑ Other: _____

Please send this form to: Professional Resource Press, PO Box 3197, Sarasota, FL 34230-3197.
You can also contact us by phone (1-800-443-3364), FAX (1-941-343-9201),
or e-mail (orders@prpress.com).